David Crookes

Facebook
for Beginners

In easy steps is an imprint of In Easy Steps Limited
16 Hamilton Terrace · Holly Walk · Leamington Spa
Warwickshire · United Kingdom · CV32 4LY
www.ineasysteps.com

Notice of Liability
Every effort has been made to ensure that this book contains accurate
and current information. However, In Easy Steps Limited and the
author shall not be liable for any loss or damage suffered by readers
as a result of any information contained herein.

In Easy Steps Limited supports The Forest Stewardship Council (FSC),
the leading international forest certification organization. All our titles
that are printed on Greenpeace approved FSC certified paper carry the
FSC logo.

MIX
Paper from
responsible sources
FSC® C020837

Printed and bound in the United Kingdom

ISBN 978-1-84078-779-5

Contents

8 Using Facebook Messenger — 105

9 Create and join events — 123

10 Using photos and video — 137

1 Introducing Facebook

Facebook was launched in 2004, and it is now the world's most popular social network.

You must be aged 13 and over if you want to sign up to Facebook.

What is Facebook?

You will have heard a lot about Facebook in day-to-day conversation, on television and in the news. It may even be the reason why you have picked up this book. But if you are still unsure what Facebook is and what it does, then you are not as alone as you may think.

Although Facebook has close to two billion active monthly users, its large and fast growth over the past decade or so means it has become different things to different people. At its heart, though, Facebook is an online social network, and it allows people to connect with friends old and new.

By signing up, you can share your experiences and thoughts, and hear those of others. You can post funny stories, photos, videos and web links. You can invite people to events and groups; buy and sell items; play games; and host video chats, too. It makes keeping in touch easier than it has ever been.

In many ways, Facebook is like a large, virtual room packed with people whose company you enjoy, and it is a great reflection of life. Indeed, the more friends you connect with, the more enjoyable and useful Facebook becomes. Once you've joined in the fun, you're likely to become hooked very quickly.

You can use Facebook on:

- **A computer**: Visit **facebook.com**

- **A mobile phone**: There are apps available for the most popular platforms.

- **A tablet**: Again, you can install apps for many such devices.

- **Your television:** There are apps available for the likes of Apple TV, allowing you to use parts of Facebook's service.

Facebook's origins

Facebook was invented by Harvard student Mark Zuckerberg and three of his classmates, Andrew McCollum, Chris Hughes and Dustin Moskovitz.

It launched on February 4, 2004 as thefacebook.com with the intention of connecting students around his university campus, and it instantly proved to be popular.

The early network allowed users to create a customized profile. Visitors to those profiles could read anything someone had posted and they could also leave messages. This struck a chord with users, who enjoyed the social aspect of the site. Within months, it was being used by students at other US universities too, and by October 2005 it had found its way to the UK as it expanded to colleges and high schools worldwide. Soon, employees at a select number of companies were also invited to join. Momentum was building fast.

Facebook eventually opened to the general public on September 26, 2006. In that same month a News Feed was introduced, and Facebook truly came into its own. The News Feed showed users a list of their friends' activity on the site, allowing for an at-a-glance view of what their connections were up to. It is a feature that remains central to Facebook today, and it has proven to be a crucial component to the network's success.

Since then lots of other features have been added, including Messenger, live streaming, and the ability to make video calls.

All of this has allowed Facebook to become one of the world's largest internet companies. As if to show Facebook's increased worth, Microsoft snapped up a 1.6 per cent share in 2007; a move which valued the company at $15 billion. Analysts say it could one day be worth as much as $1 trillion.

Facebook's key features

When you start using Facebook, you soon realize just how vast and feature-packed it is. It goes beyond simply connecting with your friends and acquaintances, even though it is packed with all the tools you need to find and hook up with others. Facebook also allows you to:

Share photos and videos

Whether you want to share a photo or video you have previously taken, or whether you wish to snap a new image or record fresh footage, Facebook lets you share the results. If the photo contains someone you know, you can associate them with the image in a process known as tagging. You can also create albums and use images to personalize your profile.

Set up and join Pages and Groups

Groups are a perfect way of bringing people together. Perhaps you are part of a football team or you run a society. Maybe you want to host  a reunion or work with others on a fundraising drive. By setting up a Group or joining one which already exists, you can get involved in discussions, kick around some ideas and collaborate with others. If, however, you want to promote a business, a cause or community association, you can set up a Page that anyone can follow. You can then keep them informed of the latest goings-on.

Keep on top of events

Quite aside from being tipped off when it's a friend's birthday, Facebook allows you to send and receive invites to specific events. As well as allowing event hosts to spread the word about an event via posts, photos and videos, it's possible to discover who can and can't attend. Facebook users can also be shown how to buy tickets.

Create a live broadcast

With Facebook Live, you can stream video footage from wherever you may be to the entire world if you wish. Available on both mobiles and via a webcam on your computer, it has become popular among celebrities, journalists, and anyone who wants to do a quick and sometimes compelling "piece to camera".

Take messaging to another level

Sure, you can use the messaging service built into your phone, but Facebook Messenger is not only convenient; it lets you contact people even if you don't have their phone number. See who is currently available, create group chats, and even engage with people direct via voice and video calls.

Challenge friends to a game

Messenger also comes with the bonus of being able to play lots of different games with a friend. You can choose from retro classics such as Pac-Man and Space Invaders, or opt to play the likes of Solitaire and Words With Friends. Try to beat their high scores.

Buy and sell items

If you have any items that you need to get rid of or if there is a something that you would love to buy, you can make good use of Facebook's Marketplace. With no fees and the ability to sell to your local community, the service gives you the tools to make and save money. It won't take up much of your time either, since the listings are both quick to create and read.

Catch the latest news

Lots of top news broadcasters and newspapers have Facebook accounts, and they regularly post links to their top stories. Lively debates are often sparked in the comment sections of these posts, and it's a great way not only to keep abreast of the latest news but gauge the mood of the public too.

Don't be afraid of trying these Facebook services. They are all free.

11

Where Facebook is heading

Facebook is continuing to innovate, ensuring that it will not stand still at any point in the near future. We know this because each year the company holds its F8 developer conference, where it outlines the technology that it is working on.

By getting to grips with Facebook today, you'll be in a position to enjoy whatever Facebook brings tomorrow. Here are some features to look forward to:

An augmented future
It has become clear that Facebook is betting big on augmented reality. This means it will look to enhance the camera on your phone and tablet by superimposing more and more data over the image you see when viewing the world through the lens of your device. Facebook says you'll be able to read restaurant reviews simply by hovering your phone in front of the building or enjoy games layered upon your real-life environment. You will even be able to leave digital objects in the augmented world that could be viewed and enjoyed by others.

A digital version of you
You may have heard of virtual reality (VR). By donning a headset that covers both of your eyes with screens, and by reacting to your head movements, you can be transported into a virtual world

that is ready to be explored. Facebook bought VR specialists Oculus Rift for a total of $2 billion, and it is working on an app called Facebook Spaces. It lets a fake cartoon-like

representation of you (called an avatar) interact with others in a virtual world.

Rise of the bots
We are already seeing the use of bots: software applications programmed to automatically perform tasks over the internet. You can chat with them in Messenger and be easily fooled into believing you are conversing with a real person. But because they

can be used to help you with your everyday tasks, and since they can second guess what you may want (some movie times, for instance), Facebook says you will be seeing a lot more of them.

Less fake news and clickbait

Fake news has become the scourge of social media. It happens when people deliberately create and share information they know to be false. It can be a misleading image, or an entire news article from a rogue website. Sometimes it can be spread by traditional media, and it is often sensationalist since it seeks to influence opinion and get you to click. Fake election news is said to have had an effect on the US presidential elections of 2016.

Facebook now has systems in place to help reduce the amount of fake news shared on its platform. It wants users to report articles that can then be independently checked. At the same time, it is using advanced algorithms to look out for exaggerated information in headlines and for signs that details are being deliberately withheld in order to encourage readers to click to find out more. The upshot is that what you read on Facebook should be much closer to the truth. You'll still have to exercise your own judgment, but it's certainly a step in the right direction.

Privacy and security

Not only does Facebook ask for personal information such as your date of birth and what you like and don't like; the social network also encourages you to share details about your life. As such, many people have raised concerns about privacy and security, and you will sometimes see articles about this in the news.

Back in 2010, Mark Zuckerberg said privacy was no longer "a social norm" and that people have become used to openly sharing information. It is true that the rise of services such as Facebook and Twitter have shifted the boundaries somewhat, yet there has also been a move towards social media that offer greater privacy and security. The likes of WhatsApp and Snapchat use technology such as end-to-end encryption and disappearing messages. These are likely to become more commonplace.

Who is Mark Zuckerberg?

As we mentioned on page 9, Mark Zuckerberg founded Facebook with the help of three classmates when he was a student at Harvard University. But he has arguably grown just as fast as the social network he created. Today he is the chairman and chief executive officer of the company, and he is said to be worth an estimated $58.6 billion. That makes him the fifth richest person in the world.

Zuckerberg's early days

Zuckerberg was born on May 14, 1984 in White Plains, New York, and he began programming computers in middle school. By the time he went to university, he had produced a program that allowed computers to communicate with each other called ZuckNet, as well as games and a media player.

Creating Facemash

In 2003, while at Harvard, he created a version of Am I Hot or Not? called Facemash. It compared many pairs of student faces and asked the user to decide who was the most stunning. Although it got him into some hot water and was pulled, it encouraged him to move on to different projects. He devoted much of his time to creating Facebook instead, eventually moving to Palo Alto, California, which is the heart of Silicon Valley.

The rise of Facebook and Zuckerberg

Zuckerberg has had many opportunities to sell Facebook but he has always turned them down, once being quoted as saying his aim was "making the world open". His efforts have seen him meeting many presidents and prime ministers as he seeks to get people communicating the world over, and he has become very well known both in and outside tech circles. He voiced himself in an episode of The Simpsons and there has also been a movie based on his founding Facebook years, called The Social Network.

Zuckerberg's generosity

In 2010, Zuckerberg signed The Giving Pledge, promising that he would, over time, give half of his wealth to charity. On top of that, he has handed far in excess of $1 billion to good causes and he is keen to help stamp out disease.

2 Setting up a new Facebook account

This chapter shows you how to open an account on Facebook, add information and a photograph, and find friends to connect with.

Getting a Facebook account

Facebook allows anyone over the age of 13 to create a single, personal account for free. The sign-up process takes very little time, and you can complete it at **facebook.com** using a web browser on your computer.

Once you have created an account, you will be also able to access it through any browser, your mobile smartphone and on any tablet you may own.

Facebook can be used on the web or via an app, and the location of settings and features can differ. We look solely at the desktop version for the first four chapters of this book, before introducing the mobile apps.

Although Facebook asks for your birthday, you will be able to control who sees it later.

1 Visit **facebook.com** and input your name, and either your mobile number or email address, on the Home screen

2 Create a password

3 Use the drop-down buttons to select your date of birth

Create an account
It's free and always will be.

First name	Surname

Mobile number or email address

New password

4 Now indicate whether you are male or female

5 Click on the **Create an account** button

Create an account

Confirm your Facebook account

1 You will need to confirm your account before you can use it. If you inputted your email address, then you will be sent a verification email. Click the **Confirm Your Account** button within the email to finish creating your account

2 Alternatively, if you inputted your mobile number, a text message containing a code will be sent to you. Enter this code in the Confirm box that appears when you log in to Facebook

Adding a profile photograph

Adding a photograph of yourself to your Facebook profile is important because it lends a personal touch. It also:

- Helps other people recognize you when you connect

- Represents you when you write posts and comments

- Encourages others to feel comfortable chatting to you

It should be the first thing you do after setting up an account. You could add an old photo, or take and use a new one.

Adding existing images via the Welcome page

1 When using Facebook for the first time, you'll find yourself on the Welcome page. Scroll down and you will see a section called **Upload a profile picture**

2 To use an existing image stored on your computer, click **Add Picture**

3 Browse the files on your computer for a saved photo, and select **Choose**. It will become your profile image

Take a photo using your webcam via the Welcome page

1 If you have a webcam, click **Take a photo**

2 You need the latest version of Adobe Flash Player installed (click **Get Flash Player** to get it). Allow Facebook to access your camera and microphone

3 Line yourself up for the shot. Click **Take photo** and then **Save** to upload it as your profile photograph

Hot tip

Close-up shots without a lot of background work best for profile images. That's because the photos display at just 170 x 170 pixels on a computer, and 128 x 128 pixels on a smartphone.

Don't forget

Profile images will be automatically cropped to fit a square.

...cont'd

Adding profile images via your Facebook Home screeen
You can also add or change your profile image from your Facebook Home screen. To reach this page, simply click on your name in the Navigation bar at the top of the screen.

1 To add an image from scratch, click **Add Photo** within the silhouetted profile in the top-left of the screen

2 Select **Upload Photo** to browse your computer for an image. When you have selected one, click **Choose**

3 You can now edit your image. Use your mouse to position it within the clear viewing area

4 You can also move the slider left and right to zoom in and out of the image

5 To describe your photo, click **Add a description...** and maybe write your name and location

6 When you have finished, click **Save**

Hot tip

Want to jolly up your profile image? Click Edit when you reposition your photograph and you can add filters, text, and even stickers.

Don't forget

When adding a profile image via the Facebook Home screen, you can take a photo using your webcam – just as you can via the Welcome page (see page 17). Simply select Add Photo as in Step 1 on the right, and then Take Photo instead of Upload Photo. Don't forget to smile for the camera.

Completing your About page

Facebook's About page allows you to write a basic profile about yourself. You can use it to share details about your life and interests, and even to let others know how they can contact you.

How much information you impart or keep private is entirely up to you. But there are benefits to giving at least some information away. Certainly, if you have a common name, providing details about your past can help others better identify you.

Adding information about yourself

You can provide an overview of your life by adding a workplace, school/university, current city, home town and relationship status.

1 Click the tab marked **About**

2 You will see that **Overview** is highlighted

3 "Plus" icons are located next to each heading. Click them if you wish to add information

4 Fill in the forms as you go down the list, ticking or unticking boxes and using any drop-down menus that you may encounter

5 When you complete each section, click **Save Changes**

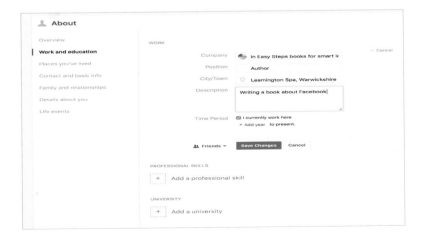

Hot tip

Select your relationship status by going to Family and Relationships. Clicking the drop-down menu lets you choose anything from single to married, to being in a civil partnership. There's an option for more complicated arrangements, too.

19

Beware

Criminals can and do attempt to use social media networks to gather other people's personal information. Next to the Save Changes box, you will find a drop-down menu that lets you choose who can view your information: the public, friends, only you, or specific people.

If you want to hide your date of birth or control who can see it, you can do so in this section. Just click the blue icons as seen in Step 3 to the right, and select how it should be displayed. You could, if you wish, just show others the day and month of your birthday. You could also choose to simply display only the year, and vice versa.

Editing your contact info

As you make your way down the sections of your About page, you should pay special attention to the **Contact and basic info** part. Here you are able to:

● Input your mobile phone number and home address

● Add your website and other social media accounts

● Make alterations to your date of birth

Adding contact information

1 On the About screen, click **Contact and basic info** on the left-hand menu

2 Click on the links for **Add a mobile phone** and **Add your address**

3 Input your details, but click the blue icon and choose who should be able to see the information from the list. Selecting **Custom** lets you be even more specific

4 Click **Save Changes**

Add a website and social link

1 The link **Add a website** lets you input a web address

2 Selecting **Add a social link** allows you to include a link to other social media profiles. These include Instagram, Twitter, Snapchat, YouTube, Pinterest, SoundCloud, Spotify, LinkedIn, Skype, and many more

3 As in Step 3 above, you can decide who can see this information on your Facebook profile. Click the button to the left of **Save changes** to do this

Upload your contacts list

Once you have completed the preparation work on your account, you'll be ready to search for friends to connect with. One of the easiest ways to do this is to upload your email contacts list to Facebook. It will then use the information to generate friend suggestions for you. To do this:

1   Go to **https://www.facebook.com/?sk=ff**

2   You will see a box to the right called **Add Personal Contacts**. Enter the email address and password of an email account that contains the greatest number of personal contacts

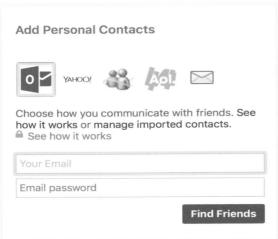

By visiting **https://www.facebook.com/invite_history.php** you can manage your invited and imported contacts. Tick the boxes next to the names of people in the displayed list, and click Delete Selected to remove any people you do not want to be listed.

21

3   Facebook will match your contacts with its database and produce a list of people you may know. Scroll down the list and tick the boxes next to the people you would like to add as a Facebook friend

4   Click **Add Friends** to send them a request

5   You will then be taken to another list of contacts; this time for people Facebook cannot find on its database. Tick the people you wish to invite, and click **Send Invitations**. An email will be sent to them, making them aware of your Facebook account

Once friends start accepting your invitations, Facebook will suggest people you may know based on mutual friends, the networks you form, your imported contacts and any other information, such as details of your workplace or where you went to school or university.

22

Manually search for friends

You can also manually look for people to connect with on Facebook using the social network's powerful search tools.

Perform a quick search

1 On any Facebook screen, click the Search bar, which contains the words **Find friends**, and type in a request

2 As you type, a list of suggestions will appear. Tap Enter on your keyboard and you will see a list of people

3 Look down the list and see if you recognize anyone from their image and/or location. If you want to connect, click **Add Friend**

4 If you are not sure you have the right person, investigate further. Click the downward arrow and look at their Photos and Interests. Select their Friends to see if you have any in common, or send them a message

Use the Advanced search facility

1 If you can't find someone by typing their name (perhaps because they've changed it) or if you want to see how many friends are listed from school, college, university, work or certain locations, click **Find Friends** at the top of the screen

Find Friends

2 To the right, you'll see the box **Search for Friends**

3 Fill in any of the text-entry boxes

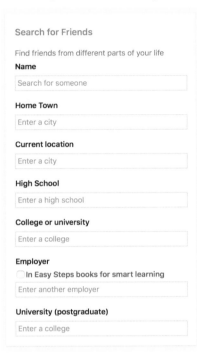

Search for Friends

Find friends from different parts of your life

Name

Search for someone

Home Town

Enter a city

Current location

Enter a city

High School

Enter a high school

College or university

Enter a college

Employer

☐ In Easy Steps books for smart learning

Enter another employer

University (postgraduate)

Enter a college

4 As you do this, a list of suggestions may appear. You can continue typing, or click a suggestion

5 Any potential friends associated with your search term will appear to the left of the screen. You can then click **Add Friend** next to anyone you want to connect with, to send an invitation

Searching via the mobile app

We have not yet looked at downloading, installing and using the Facebook apps for smartphones and tablets. But you can also search for friends on these devices.

1 Tap the **Search** bar at the top of the app, and start typing a name

2 Tap the name of a friend, and select **Add Friend**

Beware

Only connect with people that you genuinely know. If you want to become friends with a stranger, perhaps because they are famous or interesting, consider following them instead. We show you how to do this on page 28.

Hot tip

If you find there is no option to add someone as a friend, it may be because their privacy settings only let them accept requests from friends of friends. If this is the case, send them a message and ask them to invite you.

Dealing with a friend request

When someone tries to connect with you, accepting or declining their request is rather straightforward.

Accepting a friend request

1 Look for the Friends icon at the top of the screen. When a friend request is received, a red blob will appear next to it. The digit inside this blob indicates the number of requests requiring your attention

2 Click this icon, and you will be able to view the friend request. Consider whether or not you wish to accept. It is a good idea to click the contact to make sure you definitely know the person. If you wish to connect with them, select **Confirm**

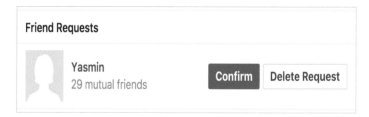

Declining a friend request

1 If you do not wish to connect with the person contacting you, simply click **Delete Request**. You do not have to give a reason for declining their invitation

2 The request will be removed from your list. But don't worry. The person sending you the friend request will not be informed that you have decided not to accept it. The only way they will know is if they check your profile in the future and see that the Add Friend option against your name is once again available

Ensuring others can find you

What if you are finding that other people are still struggling to find you? It could well be, for example, that they are searching for you using a different name.

Facebook allows you to add alternative names, such as a nickname, maiden name, alternative spelling, married name, father's name, birth name, former name, and name with title.

Adding extra names to Facebook

1 Click **About** on your profile

2 Select **Details about you** from the left-hand menu

3 Click **+ Add a nickname, a birth name...**

4 Click the drop-down menu next to **Name Type** to select the kind of name you are adding

5 Write the required name in the box next to **Name**

6 Decide whether or not you want the name to show at the top of your profile

7 Click **Save Changes**

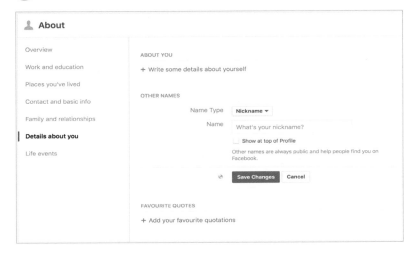

Control who can Friend you

Although the idea of Facebook is to forge links with other people, there will inevitably be some individuals who you would much rather avoid. Thankfully, there are three key ways of exerting some control over those you come across on Facebook. You can:

- Limit the people who can contact you to friends of friends

- Block individuals from contacting you

- Unfriend those you have already accepted

Limiting who can contact you

1 Click the downward arrow in the Navigation bar at the top of the screen, and select Settings

2 Look at the menu to the left of the screen, and click **Privacy**

3 You will see an option entitled **Who can contact me?** On this line, to the far right, will be the word **Edit**. Click this

4 A drop-down menu will appear. Click it, and you will see two options: Everyone and Friends of friends. Select **Friends of friends**

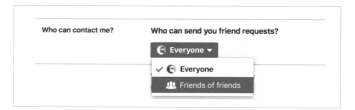

5 Click **Close**

Now, only people who are connected with your friends on Facebook will be able to send you a request. Everyone else will have to contact you direct and ask that you Friend them.

Blocking someone

Blocking is something of an extreme measure in the world of social networking. It will prevent someone from viewing anything you post, and bar them from interacting with you.

Reasons for blocking people vary, but often it is because of abusive, bullying, sexist or racist behavior. Harassment, trolling and the sharing of sexually explicit content will also cause people to block others.

Even when you block someone, you may still see their name crop up during your use of Facebook. They can appear in posts made by mutual friends or in groups and message conversations, for example. They won't, however, be able to interact with you directly.

1 Click the icon in the Navigation bar at the top of the screen

2 Select **How do I stop someone from bothering me?**

3 In the section that appears underneath, add the name or email address of the person you want to block

4 Click **Block**

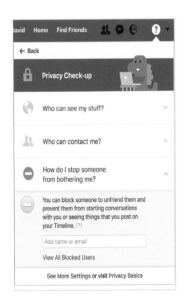

Unfriend someone

You can also decide to stop being friends with someone. The other person will not be notified.

1 Visit the person's profile

2 Hover your mouse over the Friends icon at the top of the screen to view the menu

3 Click **Unfriend**

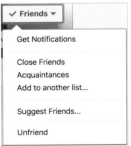

If someone has unfriended you you'll only find out if you go to their profile page, and there is an option to add them as a friend.

When you become friends with someone, you will automatically follow them.

Following other people

Facebook advises that you only become friends with people you know. But what if you want to hook up with someone who you are not on friendly terms with – a celebrity or someone in the public eye, perhaps?

For those circumstances, look for a button on their profile called Follow. Not everyone has it because it must be activated, but for those that do:

1 Click **Follow** on the profile of the person you wish to follow

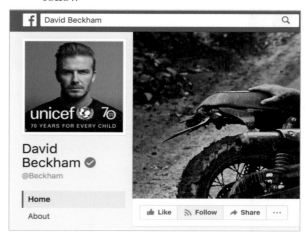

2 It will change to **Following**. To unfollow, click the arrow that will be displayed on this icon, and select **Unfollow this page**

Activate the Follow button on your profile
If you want everybody to be able to follow you, then:

1 Click the downward arrow in the top-right corner of Facebook, and choose **Settings**

2 Click **Public Posts** in the left-hand menu

3 In the top section marked **Who can follow me?** click the button marked Friends, and change it to **Public**

Beware

Allowing anyone to potentially follow you is only advisable if you intend to create posts that you want the world to see or read.

3 Familiarize yourself with Facebook

Facebook's News Feed is a key feature of the social network, since it gathers together any posts created by your friends. Here, we look at how you can view and interact with those posts.

Understanding the interface

Now that you have set up a Facebook account and begun the process of finding and adding friends, you are ready to start interacting.

There are a number of key things you can do to get the ball rolling with your account: You could:

● Read what your friends are up to.

● Write a status update or tell the world how you feel.

● Post a photograph or a video.

● Check in at your current location.

Before you do, however, it is a good idea to become familiar with the Facebook interface.

Looking at your Facebook Home screen

Your Facebook Home screen is split into various sections that run across four columns. To the left is the menu, in the middle is your News Feed, and to the right is a list of suggestions. The fourth column (not shown on this screenshot) lists your contacts and your friends' most recent activity.

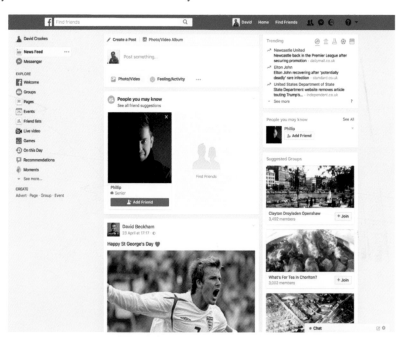

Much of your attention will be focused on the middle section.

Create a Post. This section is at the very top. You can use it to write something, and to add photos and videos to your Timeline – the place where your updates and posts are featured.

Things to do. Facebook often highlights items that it wants to bring to your attention. Here it is encouraging us to add some more friends.

Friends' posts. Running down the rest of this middle section are posts from friends, as well as people and groups that you may decide to follow.

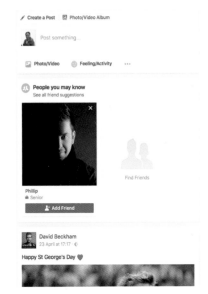

Sponsored posts are also placed within the News Feed, and it rapidly becomes a hive of activity. The more friends post and others respond, the more you'll find yourself returning to keep up with the latest gossip and news.

Using the Navigation bar to get around
You'll also find yourself using the Navigation bar at the top of the screen on many occasions. It remains constant, regardless of what page you are on.

- Clicking either the Facebook icon or Home takes you to the Home screen.

- The Search bar lets you find friends, people and groups.

- Clicking your name takes you to your Timeline.

- The icon featuring two people displays any friend requests.

- The Speech Bubble icon takes you to Messenger.

- Clicking the Globe icon shows notifications.

- The Question Mark icon offers you help.

Searching Facebook

The Search bar at the top of the Facebook screen is a powerful tool. Most people will use it to look for potential friends but it can also find Pages, Groups, posts, photographs, events and apps.

Why not try:

● Searching for a name?

● Looking for an email address?

● Inputting a telephone number?

● Making a general search using keywords?

When you search on Facebook, your search terms are saved. The most recent are displayed in a drop-down list as you type.

Searching for a specific item
Let's look for items which reflect an interest – for example, recipes.

1 Type the required keyword(s) in the Search bar

2 Click the Magnifying Glass icon, or press Enter

3 The results will appear, split into sections such as Pages, Videos, Posts from Friends, Photos, Groups, Featured Posts, News, People and Public Posts

4 Scroll down the screen and click on anything you like the look of

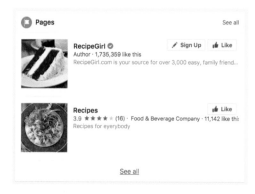

Check your News Feed

Checking your News Feed is as simple as visiting your Facebook Home screen. Use your mouse to scroll down the screen, and stop whenever you find something interesting. There are certain things to watch out for:

- Every post contains the name of the person who created it.

- Every post tells you when it was sent, either using the actual date and time, or the number of hours which have passed.

- Every post has three methods of interaction: **Like**, **Comment** and **Share**.

Playing videos

Some posts contain videos or images. Videos will automatically play without sound from within your News Feed.

If you want to hear it, simply click on the video and it will open on a new screen. Click the "x" in the top-right corner to close it.

You may see posts in your News Feed from people and Groups you have not connected with. That's because a friend will have directly interacted with them in some way.

When friends continue to Like or Comment on a post, it raises the chance of you seeing it more than once.

You can stop videos from autoplaying by clicking the downward facing arrow in the top-right corner of Facebook. Simply select Settings, click Videos in the left-hand menu, and change **Default** next to **Auto-play Videos** to Off.

Tailoring your News Feed

Hot tip

To temporarily see your News Feed in time order, click the three-dot icon next to News Feed in the left-hand menu, and select Most Recent.

What you see in your News Feed depends to a large extent on how you use Facebook. If you interact with certain people more than others, for example, then the social network's clever algorithms will make their posts a priority.

Facebook also tracks your actions, figuring out which posts you tend to engage with the most, paying careful attention to who posted it and when, the level of interactions, and the type of content. In doing so, it aims to deliver the most relevant stories for you. But that doesn't mean you can't tweak your News Feed.

Prioritize who you want to see first

1 Click the downward arrow to the far-right of the Navigation bar, and select **News Feed Preferences**

2 You will see the Preferences panel. Click **Prioritize who to see first**

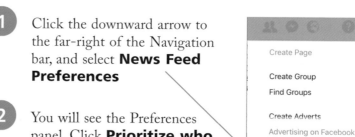

3 Click on any group or person whose posts you want to see. A star will be placed on their profile image

4 You can filter the list by clicking **All** and choosing **Friends only** or **Pages only**. **People you see first** is only useful after you've made an initial selection

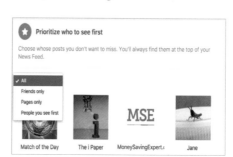

5 Click **Done**

Unfollowing people

If you decide to unfollow people, you will remain friends but you just won't see their posts in your News Feed.

1 Follow the first step on the previous page, but this time select **Unfollow people to hide their posts**

2 Click on all of the people whose posts you don't want to see any more

3 Click **Done**

4 If you need to reconnect with those people, select **Reconnect with people you've unfollowed** in the News Feed Preferences menu, and click the relevant person or Group icon

Discover Pages that match your interests

You can also tell Facebook to show posts in your News Feed from specific Pages.

1 Click **Discover Pages that match your interests** from the News Feed Preferences menu

2 Scroll down the list for potentially interesting Pages based on your interests. You'll be told if any of your connections are already following a Page. Click **Like** to see posts from it too

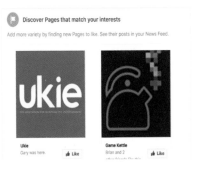

3 Click **Done**

Hide a post from your Feed

Have you come across a post you'd rather not see or a post that keeps cropping up over and over again? You can hide it from your News Feed.

1 Look for a downward-pointing arrow in the top right-hand corner of the post, and click it

2 Select **Hide post**

Report a post, image or video

If a post is offensive or you feel it breaches your privacy, you can report it:

1 Click the downward arrow on the post

2 Select the option to **Report**

3 State why you don't like it, click **Continue** and follow the suggestions, or call for more information

Commenting on a post

Facebook encourages you to respond to posts made by other people, and the ability to comment appears beneath each one. Be aware, though, that if you comment on a post that is Public, it can be read by anyone online – not just those in your social circle. If you comment on a friend's post, their privacy settings regarding the post will also affect who can read it.

Writing a comment

1 Underneath a post, you will see a button called **Comment**. Click it whenever you want to leave a reply to something you have read, seen or watched

2 Compose your message in the text box that contains the words **Write a comment...**

3 Press **Enter** on your keyboard to post it

4 Your comment will appear beneath the post for others to read. To get involved in a conversation, you can click **Reply** beneath anyone else's comment. Comments can be edited and deleted, and you are also free to write as many as you wish

Post a sticker

1 For those who believe a picture paints a thousand words, there are stickers. Click the **smiley face** in the Comment text box

2 Look through the categories, from Happy to Confused, and choose a sticker. Click **+** if you want to look through the Sticker store. Select a sticker to post it

You can mention (or "tag") a person in a post. Just type their name and select them from a list. They will be notified that you have tagged them. See page 139 for more on this.

If you like stickers, keep checking the Sticker Store since there are sometimes updates surrounding holidays and movie releases.

As well as selecting a sticker, you can also choose and send a GIF in Facebook comments. Click the GIF button in the Comment text box.

Don't forget

Much of the fun of Facebook is interacting with others and seeing people react to you, so don't be afraid to get stuck in.

Reacting to a post

Reading posts is all well and good, but you're bound to have a burning desire to react to something a friend or group has written, uploaded or created. It used to be that Facebook only allowed you to Like a post, but now there is a range of five other reactive emotions:

Expressing a reaction to someone's post

1 Beneath a post you will see an option called **Like**. You can simply click this if you do indeed like something you see

2 Alternatively, hover your mouse over **Like** without clicking it, and more reactions will appear. Choose between **Love**, **Haha**, **Wow**, **Sad** and **Angry**, depending on how the post makes you feel

3 Your name will appear alongside your reaction within the post. You will also be able to see if and how others have reacted to the post too

4 An entry will appear on your Timeline to say you have reacted to a post, and the person who created it will also be notified of your interaction

5 If you change your mind or if you've clicked the wrong reaction, go back and select something different

6 To remove a reaction entirely, just click the one you've currently selected

Posting photos or videos

As well as becoming involved in an interesting debate, reminiscing or sharing a few jokes, you can also share photos or videos in the Comment section of a post.

- Videos or photos can help you to advance an argument or illustrate a point.

- They can inject some humor into the comments of a post.

- They can also encourage lots of other sharing and make your comment stand out.

To post a photo or a video:

1 Look for the Camera icon to the right within the Comment text box. Click on this in order to post both videos and photos

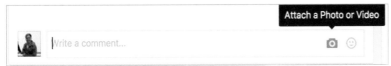

2 Browse through the media stored on your computer for a photo or video to share

3 Click **Open**

4 Press **Enter** on your keyboard to post it

5 Other people will now be able to interact with your photo or video, leaving comments of their own or reacting to it with a Like or one of the other reactions

6 If you decide that you want to remove the video or photo, just click the Pencil icon and select **Delete** from the drop-down menu that appears

You can write text alongside your photo or video to help explain or contextualize it.

You can tag people in photos (see page 48 for more on this). When you tag someone in a photo you upload, that person will be notified. Depending on their privacy settings, their friends may be able to see the image, Like it, or make a comment.

Hot tip

When hovering over a Trending topic, you can click the x in the top corner to remove it from the list.

See what is Trending

Although you can engage with your friends and follow groups, celebrities and public figures, you are not confined to your own Facebook bubble. The social network can also be a useful way of seeing what is happening in the outside world and gauging what is getting people talking.

Look down the third column of the Facebook Home screen and you will see a section called Trending. Here you are able to discover popular topics among Facebook's users. Every included topic is there because lots of publishers are writing about it and because a good number of people are engaging with the content.

Facebook says it has a team which reviews this section. It helps to eliminate abuse by people who may seek to artificially inflate the importance of a topic.

What categories does it include?
There are five categories in total:

- Top trends

- Politics

- Science and Technology

- Sports

- Entertainment

> Trending
>
> ↗ **Newcastle United**
> Newcastle back in the Premier League after securing promotion - dailymail.co.uk
>
> ↗ **Nestlé**
> Nestlé to axe nearly 300 jobs and move Blue Riband production to Poland - telegraph.co.uk
>
> ↗ **Ivanka Trump**
> Ivanka Trump meets Angela Merkel in Berlin - telegraph.co.uk
>
> ▾ See More   ?

Viewing the topics

1 Click on one of the category icons at the top of the Trending box

2 Hover over the blue link for each entry to read a brief description of the topic

3 Click the blue link to see the story, a selection of posts, and any photos and videos

4 **Like** Pages and posts, or compose comments as you scroll down the screen

4 Creating your first Facebook posts

This chapter explains how you can create your own posts, bring them to the attention of others, and make use of photos and videos.

If you use your post to ask for advice on where to eat or go, you will be prompted to turn on the Recommendations feature. If you do so, then when your friends respond, Facebook will add addresses, photos and reviews. The recommendations can be viewed in one place by going to https:// www.facebook.com/ recommendations

42

Creating a written post

Although reading, seeing and reacting to what others are posting is entertaining enough, very soon you will want to spark your own conversations. You do this by creating a post, and the simplest of these involves writing a few words about what you are up to, or getting something off your chest.

1 Go to the Homepage or your Timeline

2 At the top of the second column, you will see a box containing the words **What's on your mind?**

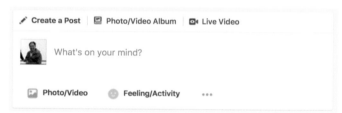

3 Click the box, and a window will appear

4 You can now write anything you wish in this box

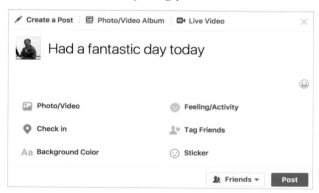

5 Click the drop-down menu labeled **Friends**. Select who should see your post: anyone, just friends, or a select few. See pages 26-27 for more details

6 When you are finished, click **Post**

Expressing your feelings

No, we're not about to sit you down on the couch and ask you to express your inner thoughts. Instead, we're going to show you how you can share your current mood or better get across what you are currently doing or want to do.

1 Click the icon for **Feeling/Activity** within the Create a Post box. Now click it again

Feeling/Activity

2 A list of categories will appear, ranging from Feeling, Celebrating and Thinking about to Listening to, Playing and Traveling to. Scroll down the list to see them all

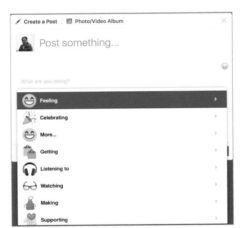

3 Select the category you want to use and scroll down the next list which appears, to view all of the available options. Choose the feeling or activity that you want to express. Some ask you to describe your feeling or activity

4 The feeling or activity will then appear within your post. You can write something in relation to it if you wish

5 When you are finished, click **Post**

6 Your friends will be able to view this extra piece of information within your post

Many security experts urge caution when using this feature since it could reveal when you're not at home or, if you are, where you live.

Checking into a location

If you want to include a location in your post, you can "check in". Facebook will look for an identifiable place.

1 In the Create a Post box, click the icon for **Check in**

2 A drop-down list will suggest potential locations. If your location is there, click it

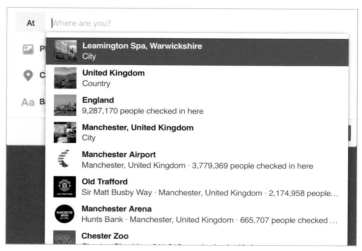

3 If it is not listed, you can simply write your current location in the **At** text box. More suggestions will be made as you type

4 You can now write something (or leave it blank) and select **Post** when you have finished. Your post will be accompanied by a map pinpointing your location for others to see

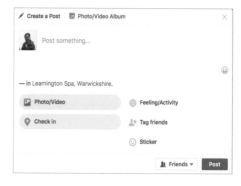

Tagging your friends in posts

A popular method of connecting with people who are already friends with you is to tag them in your posts. Doing this produces a link to their profile, which anyone who sees it is able to view. Your post may also appear on your friend's Timeline, widening the number of people who will see it.

1 Click the icon for **Tag friends** within the Create a Post box

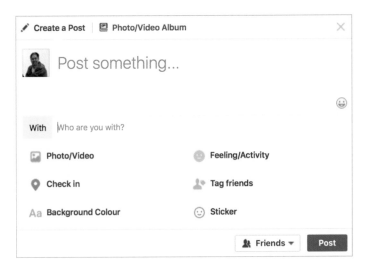

2 In the box marked **With**, write the name of the person you want to tag. As you do this, a list of suggestions will appear. Select the person you want

Any friends you tag will be notified of your action. It can be worthwhile asking them whether they mind you tagging them before you do it.

3 Their name will now appear in your post

4 If you want to tag more than one person, you can simply repeat the process with another name in the same box

5 Write something, and click **Post** when you have finished

6 A clickable link bearing their name will appear in your post when it becomes viewable on Facebook

Selecting who sees your posts

Facebook allows you to control who is able to see your posts. You can do this on a post-by-post basis. What you choose is very much down to you and the content that you are looking to share.

Don't forget

The setting you choose remains in place for all subsequent posts until you change it again.

1 In the Create a Post box, click the icon for **Friends**

2 You will see a number of options in the drop-down menu which appears. After writing a post, you can:

Don't forget

If you tag someone in a post, they will be able to control how the post will appear on their Timeline.

- **Make it Public.** This allows anyone to see what you have posted, whether or not they are using Facebook.

- **Allow your friends to see it.** Those you have added as a friend will see the post in their News Feeds.

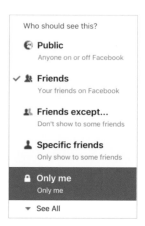

- **Exclude some friends from seeing it.** This will stop it from appearing in certain friends' News Feeds.

- **Let specific friends see it.** Only those on your list will read or see your posts.

- **Keep it to yourself.** It'll be solely for your eyes.

3 Click **More** to see all of the options, and select the one that best suits your post

4 If you decide to limit your post to certain friends, then you'll be shown a list of your connections. Add or remove people who you do and don't want to see your post, before clicking **Save Changes**

5 Click **Post** to send it on its way

Enhancing your posts

If you want to make your posts more eye-catching, there are three good ways of doing this: changing the background color of your post, adding stickers or using an emoji.

Changing the background color

1 Click on the Create a Post box and select the icon for **Background Color**

2 You will see a row of colors appear beneath the text section. Click one of the circles and the background will change to that color

Spellings are localized.

Adding stickers

1 Click on the icon for **Sticker**

2 Select one of the emotions, ranging from Happy to Eating to Sleepy

3 Choose an image to be inserted into your post

Clicking on the **+** icon when choosing a sticker will open the Sticker Store, giving you even more selections to choose from.

Adding an emoji

1 Click the smiley face in the bottom right-hand corner of the text section

2 You will see lots of images of smileys. These are examples of emoji. Choose a category at the bottom of the box

3 Select an emoji

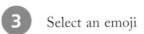

Posting a photo or video

As well as posting text, you are also able to post photos and videos. Uploading images and videos is a great way of sharing your day-to-day activities. You can post media that you own yourself, or media that you find online.

Posting your own photographs and videos

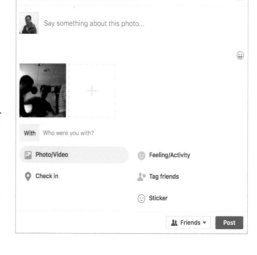

1 When you are ready to post a photo or video, click the **Photo/Video** icon in the Create a Post box at the top of the screen

2 Browse your computer for the photograph or video you want to upload

3 To add more photos, click the **+** icon, and browse your computer for more images or videos

4 You can write some words about the photo or video. Click **Post** to upload

Identifying friends in a photograph
If you want to identify who is in the photograph with you:

1 Click the image within the Create a Post box before you upload it

2 Facebook will pick on any people in the picture and ask you to write their name in the text entry boxes

Posting photos you find online

When surfing the web, you are bound to come across interesting and funny photographs. You may like to share these with your friends on Facebook. Doing so is very easy:

1 Right-click a photograph you like on a web page

Hot tip

You can also copy a web address generated by YouTube after pressing Share, and manually paste it into a post.

2 Look for an option that allows you to copy an image address. This varies from computer to computer and browser to browser, but the choices can include Copy Image Address, Copy Image Location or Copy Image URL, or even a straightforward Copy

3 Right-click in the Create a Post box on Facebook, and select Paste. The image will now appear

4 Write some accompanying text, and click **Post**

Posting a video you find online

Many video websites allow you to share their content on social media. YouTube, for example, has a dedicated Share button which produces a link that you can use.

1 Visit **youtube.com** and look for a video

2 Click the Share icon beneath it

Hot tip

If you want to share a specific point in a video, YouTube has an option that lets you choose a start time. You'll see it under the web address in YouTube's Share box.

3 Select the icon for Facebook, and a Post window will open. The video will be automatically included

4 Write your message, and click **Post to Facebook**

If you only want to share the content of a post and not the message that accompanies it, untick the box for Include Original Post.

Hot tip

Enhance your shared post by adding a location, tagging others, using emojis or choosing a picture to indicate how you feel. The options appear at the bottom of the Share window.

Sharing someone else's post

You will often come across a post that you would like to share with others. Luckily, every post comes with a Share option. It allows you to share links with anybody you wish. You won't, however, be able to widely share images, videos, or status updates by a friend, if their privacy settings restrict their posts to a specific audience. Here is how to share posts:

1   Click the option for **Share** underneath a post

2   Select how you want to share it. You can:

- **Share Post Now (Friends)**. This instantly shares the post and does not give you an opportunity to comment on it.

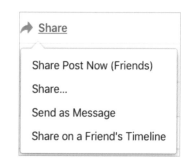

- **Share**. You will have the option to write something too.

- **Send as Message**. Posts can be sent direct and privately to one person via Facebook Messenger (see Chapter 8).

- **Share on a Friend's Timeline**. Use if you want to bring it to someone's attention publicly.

3   If clicking **Share**, you can select **Share on your own Timeline** and change it to **Share in a group** or **Share in an event**. We'll cover Groups and events later in the book. In all cases, write something about the post

4   If clicking **Share on a Friend's Timeline**, write the name of your friend in the window that appears

5   Click **Post**

Editing your posts

When you create a post, it is not set in stone. Sometimes you'll look at it and spot a mistake, or you'll wish you hadn't put it up. Facebook allows for such eventualities by letting you edit, and even delete, posts. You can also change the date of the post and hide it from your Timeline.

Make changes to a post

1 To edit a post – perhaps correcting mistakes such as the bad spelling of State below – click the downward arrow in the top-right corner and select **Edit Post**

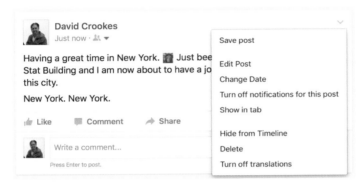

David Crookes
Just now ·

Having a great time in New York. Just bee
Stat Building and I am now about to have a jo
this city.

New York. New York.

Like   Comment   Share

Write a comment...
Press Enter to post.

Save post

Edit Post
Change Date
Turn off notifications for this post
Show in tab

Hide from Timeline
Delete
Turn off translations

2 The post will appear in a new window, allowing you to change the text, add or remove images and videos, tag people, include an emoji, and check in. You can also change who can see your post and remove the location

3 Click **Save** when you have finished editing

Changing the date

1 If you want to alter the date of your post, click the downward arrow and select **Change Date**. Use the drop-down options to alter the year, month and day

2 Click **+Add hour** to change the time

3 Click **Save**

Simply click Delete from the drop-down menu and confirm to remove an unwanted post.

If you don't want a post to appear on your Timeline, select Hide from Timeline. The post will still appear in your friends' News Feeds, unless you delete it altogether.

Turning off notifications for a post means Facebook won't let you know if someone responds to it.

Use the Filters when searching to narrow down the amount of information you can see.

View your activity log

Everything that you post and share is logged by Facebook, but you are able to see a list of your activities and manage it.

1 Click the downward arrow in the top-right corner of any Facebook page. You will see it in the blue bar

Create Page

Create Group
Find Groups

Create Adverts
Advertising on Facebook

Activity Log
News Feed Preferences
Settings
Log out

2 Select Activity Log. It will have a number next to it, showing how many posts you've been tagged in

3 Look down the list. By pressing the **Edit** (pen) icon to the far-right of an entry, you can make a change. For example, you can unlike a post or hide it from your Timeline

4 To see which posts have tagged you, click **Review X items**, where X is the number of items you can review

5 To remove a tag, click the downward arrow in the top-right corner of a post and select **Remove Tag**

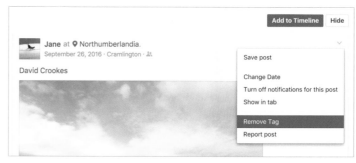

5 Start using the Facebook app

As well as accessing Facebook via a browser on your computer, you can also check your News Feed, search for friends, and engage with others using an app on a mobile device. This is great for keeping in touch with others, no matter where you may be.

Don't forget

You can also visit **facebook.com** in any browser (such as Safari or Chrome) on any mobile device.

Download the Facebook app

So far, we have looked at accessing Facebook via a browser on a computer. This, however, is only one way of enjoying the services that the social network provides.

More than half of all users access the service only on a mobile device. That means they are using their smartphones and tablet computers as the sole method of creating posts, checking their News Feeds, enjoying videos, and so much more.

Since more than 80 per cent of us are now said to own a smartphone or tablet, there's a good chance that you will want to use Facebook on a mobile device too. Just like the website, there is no charge for doing this. You can open a browser on your phone and visit **facebook.com** to access a website specifically tailored for mobile use, or you can download a dedicated app.

Downloading the Facebook app for Apple iOS
The app is available for Apple's iOS operating system, which means it can be downloaded and installed for the iPhone, iPod touch and iPad.

1 Open the App Store on your iOS device by tapping its icon on your Home screen

2 In the Search bar at the top of the screen, type **Facebook** and tap **Search**

3 It should appear as the first search result. You can tap the entry to read more about it if you wish but to download it, tap **Get**

4 Enter your Apple ID password, and the app will download to your device

5 Tap **Open** to launch it. In future, look for the icon on your Home screen and tap that

Downloading the Facebook app for Android

Android is currently the most popular mobile operating system, so it will come as no surprise to learn that you download Facebook to any smartphone or tablet which runs it.

1 Open the Play Store app on your Android device by tapping the icon on your phone or tablet's Home screen

2 In the Search bar at the top of the screen, type **Facebook** and tap the Magnifying Glass icon

3 If you want to immediately install Facebook, tap the **Install** button in the search result for the social network.

You can also tap More Info and read details about it. There is an Install button on that page too

4 As long as you are logged into Google on your device, it will install

5 Go to your Home screen by tapping the on-screen Home button. Look for and tap the Facebook icon in the applications tray of your device to open it

There is also a Facebook app available for Amazon's Kindle Fire tablets. Find it at https://www.amazon.com/Facebook/dp/B0094BB4TW

Hot tip

If you can't remember your login details, you can also click Forgot Password when logging in via a browser on your computer.

Log in to the Faceboook app

With the app installed on your device, it is time to log in.

1 Open the mobile app for the first time, and you will be asked to log in using the email address or phone number that you always use to access your account

2 If you have forgotten your password, simply tap **Forgot Password?** and it will seek to verify your identity before allowing you to input a new one

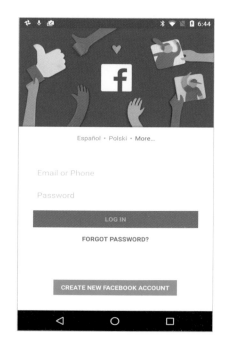

3 You will be asked if you wish to save your login details on your device so that you do not always have to keep entering it whenever you open the app

4 Facebook will also ask whether or not you want to allow it to access your location. This, it says, allows certain features to work properly

Logging out of the Facebook app

1 If you need to log out of the app, tap the **Menu** button (you will find this in the bottom-right corner of the iOS and Windows Phone Facebook apps and in the top-right corner of the Android app)

2 Scroll to the very bottom of this page and you will see an option to **Log Out**. Simply tap this. You'd need to re-input your username and password next time you try to access the Facebook app

Understanding the interface

When you start using Facebook on your mobile device, whether a smartphone or tablet, it will default to your News Feed. This allows you catch up with the latest gossip, news and videos when you're on the move. But what can you see on the screen? Here are some of the basics:

Pull down on the screen when viewing the News Feed to refresh it.

Take a photo. Snap an image using the camera on your device.

Perform searches. Find various things on Facebook.

Write a post. Create text and photo/video posts. This section is similar to the one you see on the computer browser version of Facebook.

Various posts from others. Use your finger to scroll down this screen and view posts created by others. Leave a reaction, make a comment or share any posts you enjoy.

Explore other areas of Facebook. These icons take you to other sections and features on the social network.

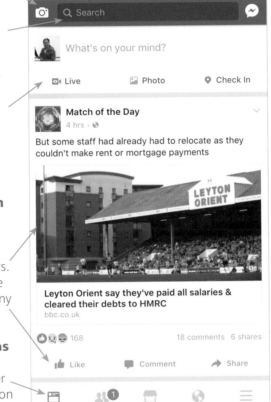

57

Other versions

We have pictured the iOS version above, but other versions differ ever so slightly.

The Android version, for example, has some of its key features placed on the screen in a slightly different order.

This is due to the positioning of the Android buttons at the bottom of the screen.

Viewing your own profile

As we've just seen, the Facebook app will take you direct to your News Feed by default. But you can view your own profile too.

1 Tap the Menu icon. You will see this in the bottom right-hand corner of the iOS app and in the top right-hand corner of the Android app

2 Select **View your profile**

Looking at your profile on iOS

Profile image. Your current image will be positioned at the top of the profile page. You can tap Edit to change it.

Pending Posts. Any posts involving you which are subject to review are flagged up.

Write a Post. Create text and photo/video posts.

Update Info. You can make amends to your bio.

Activity Log. Get the full lowdown on how you are using Facebook.

More. Selecting this allows you to change your profile image, the cover photo at the top of the screen, and view privacy shortcuts.

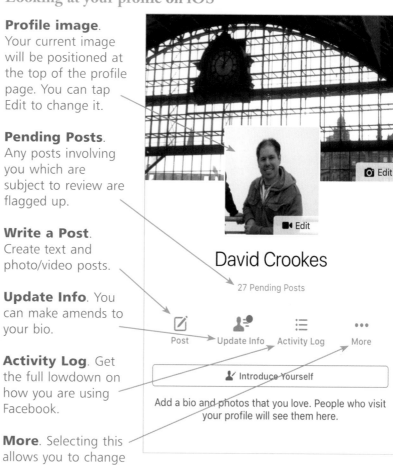

Looking at your profile on Android

Search your posts. A Search bar is located at the top of your profile page.

Profile image. The image you are currently using will be located here, beneath your cover image. Both can be edited.

Pending Posts. If you need to review any posts, they will be flagged up.

Update Info. You can make amends to your bio.

More. Change your profile or cover image, view privacy shortcuts or copy a link to your profile.

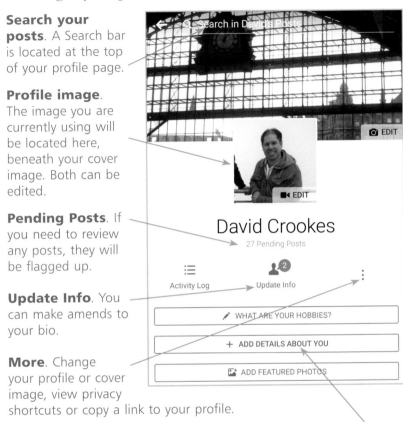

Requested info. If Facebook believes some key information is missing from your profile, it will request it.

Other important information on your profile

As you continue to scroll down the screen, you will see a few other sections. You will be able to:

- View any photos you have posted or uploaded.

- Review the personal information held on your profile.

- See how many friends you have, check their profiles and check out how many new posts they have created.

- View, edit and even delete your own posts.

If you are looking for a post you can tap Filter, which will help narrow down the search by date, person posting and tags.

Finding friends and more

You can use the search engine within the app to quickly look for friends. This search engine can also be used to find posts, videos, Pages, photos, places, Groups, apps and events, just as it can on the computer version of Facebook.

1 Tap the Search bar at the top of the screen

2 Begin typing your search term

3 As you type, Facebook will make suggestions. You can stop typing at any time and tap one of those suggestions

4 You can also continue typing and tap **Search** when you are finished

5 The results page will be displayed. If you are looking for a friend, you will find them under the People tab. You can also tap the tabs for the other categories if you are looking for something other than a person

6 When you have found someone you wish to add, simply tap their name

7 You will be taken to their profile page. Ensure you have the right person, and tap **Add Friend**

8 A friend request will be sent to the person. Now sit back and wait for them to agree. You will then automatically become Facebook friends

Checking friend requests

When people try to become friends with you on Facebook, their requests appear within the app. You can accept or decline them.

1 Tap the Friends button at the top or the bottom of the screen, depending on which smartphone or tablet operating system you are using

2 Look under the section marked **Friend Requests** for any entries

3 If people are trying to contact you, there will be two options next to their photo and name: Confirm and Delete

4 If you wish to accept a person as a friend, tap **Confirm** to add them

5 If you do not want to accept a request, tap **Delete**. The person will be removed from the list and the request will be denied

Checking Facebook's friend recommendations

Facebook will look for any mutual friends you have and promote them as potential people you may want to add.

1 Look under the section marked **People You May Know**

2 If there is a list of names, you'll be told how many mutual friends you share with each person

3 Decide whether to **Add Friend** to send them a request to connect or **Remove**, in which case they will be taken off your list

When deciding whether to activate notifications on Android, decide if you want them to show without a sound or vibration. You can also allow them to appear when Do Not Disturb is turned on.

Hot tip

On iOS, as well as turning notifications on and off, you can also indicate how you would like them to appear and whether or not you want them to make a sound.

Accessing your notifications

When somebody adds something to Facebook that you are likely to be interested in, you will get a notification. This could indicate:

- **A mention**: Your name may be included in somebody's post.

- **A reaction**: A comment on a post you're involved with.

- **Something new on a Page/Group you're following**: You'll be kept informed of new posts, photos and videos.

- **A new event**: Events added by someone you are following.

- **A shared link**: Links posted to Pages and Groups you follow.

1 On a smartphone or tablet, tap the Globe icon

2 Tap any notification to view it in full

3 Read notifications will turn from blue to white

Allowing and disallowing push notifications
To be kept informed of Facebook notifications when you are not using the app, allow alerts or messages to be sent to your device.

1 **For Android**: Go to the Settings app on your device

2 Go to **Applications** and navigate to Apps > Facebook > Notifications

3 Use the top button to turn notifications on or off

4 **For iOS**: Go to the Settings app

5 Tap **Notifications** and then tap Facebook

6 Use the button next to **Allow Notifications** to turn the notifications on and off

Adjusting your notifications

To prevent you being bombarded by notifications, you can decide on the kind of alerts that you want to receive on your device.

Using Android

1 Tap the Menu icon within the Facebook app

2 Tap **App Settings** and select **Notifications**

3 Use the sliders next to each of the entries. The top section deals with how the notifications are received. The bottom section lets you decide which notifications you want to see. Options include wall post, comment and photo tag alerts

4 Tap each option to decide whether or not to activate

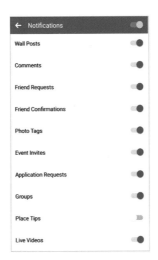

Using iOS

1 Tap the Menu icon within the Facebook app

2 Scroll down, tap **Settings** and select **Account Settings**

3 Tap **Notifications**

4 Tap items in the bottom section to decide the kind of notifications you want to receive. They include close friends' activity, birthday alerts and Group posts

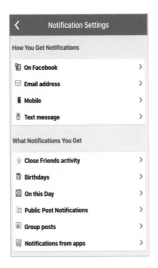

You can determine who should see your post by clicking **Friends** underneath your name in the status update box.

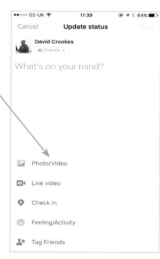

Hot tip

If you start to create a post, then decide you want to continue it later, tap the backward-facing arrow in Android, or **Cancel** in iOS, and choose **Save Draft**. The next time you attempt to write a status update, your previous message will appear again.

Creating a post via the app

You can create posts on both your computer (see page 42) and on the app. As well as writing a text-based post, you can upload a photo or video, check in, express a feeling or activity, tag friends, and even create a live video.

All of Facebook's cross-platform apps work in much the same way.

1. Tap the status update box

2. Select the type of post you wish to create from the menu which appears beneath the main text-entry window

3. If you simply want to write a text-based post, tap **What's on your mind?** in order to call up the on-screen keyboard

4. You can then change the background color using the colored circles

5. You can also add photos and videos, check in, or choose a feeling or activity by selecting one of the icons at the bottom of the text window

6. When you have completed your status update, tap **Post** in the top right-hand corner. It will now be posted to your Timeline, where it can be read by other people in their News Feeds

Adding photos and videos

Your smartphone or tablet will be packed with images and videos. You can share any of these in your posts, or take a fresh photo or video using your device's camera.

Using an existing image

1 Tap the status update box in Android and select **Photo/Video**. If you are using iOS, you can directly tap **Photo** in the status update box

2 You will be shown all of the images and videos that are saved on your device. Scroll down and select the one you wish to use

3 Tap **Done** and it will be added to a post

4 Write a message and, when complete, tap **Post**

Using a simple, fresh image or video

1 Follow Step 1 above but tap the Camera icon in the top-left corner of iOS, or choose either the Camera or Video Recorder icon in the top-right corner of Android

2 Your device's camera will be activated. Tap the large circular button at the bottom of the screen to snap an image or record some video (in iOS you will see options for an image or video either side of this). If recording video, pressing the button again will stop filming

3 Tap the blue Tick icon in Android, or select Use in iOS to place your taken image or video into a post

4 Write a message, and tap **Post** when you're finished

Hot tip

You will also notice a Camera icon in the top left-hand corner of your app's News Feed. This can produce some very snazzy images and videos. We'll look at this in greater detail in Chapter 10.

Checking in via the app

Since mobile devices are made to be taken with you when you are out and about, the Facebook app makes it easy for you to check in at a location and let others know where you are. As with the desktop version of this feature, you'll need to bear in mind the potential privacy and security concerns, but it's a nice way to bring your posts to life.

Turn on Location Services

Before you can use this feature, you must have Location Services turned on.

1. Go to your device's **Settings** app

2. In Android, select **Location**, while in iOS select **Privacy** and tap **Location Services**

3. At the top of the screen on both  iOS and Android, you will see a slider button. Turn it **On**

4. You now need to specifically allow the Facebook app to access your location. You can do this in iOS by scrolling down the screen and tapping Facebook, before selecting either **While Using the App** or **Always**

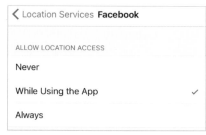

5. In Android, you need to go back to the main page of the Settings app. Once there, tap **Apps** and select the **cog** icon at the top of the screen. Then, tap **App Permissions** and select **Location** before looking down the list for Facebook and turning the slider **On**

6. For these changes to activate, you must now restart the Facebook app. You will be able to start using the Check In feature on your mobile device

Checking in to a location

If you are in a location that you wish to share with your friends or the wider Facebook population, you can check in.

1 When using iOS, tap the button for **Check In**, which you will see in your status update box

2 When using Android, tap the status update box and then select **Check In** from the list of options at the bottom of the screen

3 Scroll down and select a location (the Android and iOS screens look similar)

You can add a location to an existing post. Click the downward arrow in the corner of your post, and select Edit.

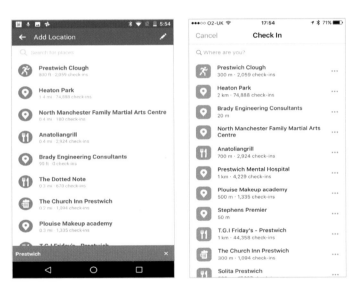

4 You can now tag any friends you are with, or anyone else that you wish to alert to your location. Scroll down the list and tap their names. Otherwise, tap **Skip**

5 The location will be added to your post, and you can write a message or add photos. When you're ready, simply tap **Post**

Altering the app permissions

Over time, Facebook will seek to access various components of your device. You can review these and stop Facebook from accessing them.

Beware

Turning off some of the permissions can affect the smooth running of Facebook. Turning off access to the camera, for example, will prevent you taking new photos and videos via the app.

Android

1 Go to your device's **Settings** app, scroll down and select **Apps**. Then look for the entry for **Facebook**

2 Select **Permissions**

3 Review the permissions Facebook has been granted and turn off any that you are not happy with, using the sliders

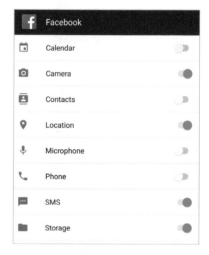

iOS

1 Go to the **Settings** app, scroll quite far down the list, and select **Facebook**

2 Tap **Settings**

3 In the section **Allow Facebook To Access** use the sliders to turn off any permissions that you do not want Facebook to have

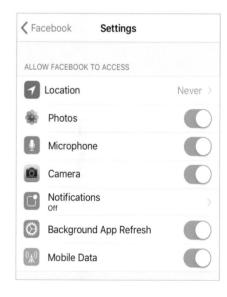

6 Working with Groups

If you have a particular interest, then you may well find there is a Facebook Group full of like-minded people. If there isn't, then you may want to set one up yourself. Facebook Groups allow you to discuss your favorite topics with others; share files, photos and videos; and foster a strong community. Facebook is also giving them greater prominence in a bid to bring the world closer together.

You can also find and join Groups on a mobile device. Click the three-bar Menu button, select Groups, and look under the Discover tab.

Don't forget

Some Groups are public and others are closed. Your Facebook friends may also see you have joined a Group.

Joining a Facebook Group

Facebook Groups offer a wonderful way of bringing together people with a common interest. They allow members to share posts, photos, videos and documents, and they can also be made private. You can use them for:

- Organizing a party or a special occasion.

- Discussing interesting topics, ranging from photography and politics to gardening and gaming.

- Working together on a project at work or in the community.

- Buying and selling specific items, and much, much more.

Find and join a Group
It is easy to explore the different Groups that exist, and join them.

1 Click **Groups** in the left-hand menu on your computer. You will find it listed under Explore

2 Select a category running from the top of the screen, or scroll to view suggested Groups. If your friends are involved with a Group, their profile image will be displayed

3 To immediately request access, click **+Join**. Otherwise, click its name

4 Group pages contain a description. To join a Group, click **+Join Group**

5 Many Groups are private so you won't always see posts, photos and other content from the Group until your join request is accepted by the Group's administrators

Engaging with a Group

Whether you have joined a public or closed Group, you are able to engage with the other members and even send invites to others.

Creating a post

You can write a post, upload a photo or video, express your feeling and an activity, check in and tag friends, just as you can when writing a post that you want to appear on your own Timeline.

1 Visit the Group that you wish to engage with

2 Use the box at the top to create your post

3 Ensuring the name of the Group is shown, click **Post**

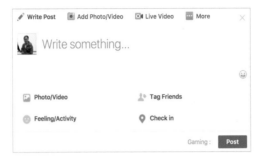

Commenting on other members' posts

When scrolling through the posts created by members, you may want to Like or Share a post. You may also want to leave a comment. You do this in the same way that you would with any post you come across (see page 37).

Using a mobile device

Navigate to the Group that you wish to engage with by tapping the three-bar Menu button in the app and selecting Groups. You can scroll through the Group in the same way as you would scroll through your News Feed, liking, sharing and commenting on posts that interest you. See page 57 for more details.

If you invite people to join a closed Group, the administrator may have to grant approval before they are accepted.

Facebook will also suggest Groups for you to join based on those your friends are members of, and any pages you have liked.

Send and receive invitations

If you know a Facebook user who may like to become a member of a Group that you have joined, you can send them an invite.

1 Locate the Add Members box

2 Enter their name or email address

3 Click the Note icon to personalize the invite

4 Click **Invite**

Receiving an invite

When you send an invite to someone, they have the option of joining or declining. You can also be invited to a Group.

1 Anyone invited to join a Group is sent a notification

2 Click **Groups** in the left-hand menu of Facebook to see any you have been sent

3 Select the **Groups** tab at the top of the screen

4 You will see Pending Invites. Select **Join** or **Decline**

What if you are automatically added to a group?
If administrator approval is not needed in order to add members, then you may find you have been added without your permission. In this case, you'll need to leave the group.

1 After receiving a notification saying you have been added, go to the group and click **Joined**

2 Select **Leave Group** and you will be removed from the member list. You'll no longer be notified of any updates from the group

Altering your notifications

By default, every time somebody posts to a Group, you will receive a notification.

The only exception is when a Group has more than 250 members. In that case, in order to prevent you from being pestered by notifications, Facebook will only inform you of suggested posts and posts from your friends. They appear when you click or tap the Globe icon.

If you are receiving too many notifications from a Group and you would like to reduce the number, you can select one of three alternative options. These include turning them off.

1 Visit the Group that you want to alter the notifications for

2 Click **Notifications** towards the top of the screen

3 Selecting **All Posts** will ensure you get a notification every time a member creates a post in the Group

4 Selecting **Highlights** will only show posts from your friends and suggested posts

5 Selecting **Friends' Posts** will notify you only when a friend posts

6 Selecting **Off** deactivates the notifications for that particular Group. You will see and receive notifications of replies to any posts you create in the Group however, and you will also continue to receive notifications from both other Groups and sections of Facebook

Hot tip

You can make use of up to 10 poll options.

Creating a Group poll

Setting up a poll lets you gauge the opinion of other members in a group. If the group is about a particular genre of music, for instance, you could ask people to choose from a selection of bands. Or, if the group concerns a birthday party, group members could vote on the most suitable venue.

1 Go to a group and click **More** in the Create a Post box

2 Select **Create Poll**

3 Type your question where it says **Ask Something**

4 Click **Add an option...**

5 Type your first option before clicking **Add an option...** on the next lines to create extra poll choices

6 Click **Poll Options**

7 To allow members to add their own poll options, tick the first box

✓ Allow anyone to add options
✓ Allow people to choose multiple options

8 Tick the second box to let group members choose more than one option in your poll

9 Click **Post**

Creating a Group document

Writing a standard post will suffice most of the time, but you may want to collaborate with Group members on a document. Facebook lets you create a document that others can read and edit.

1 Go to a Group and click **More** in the Create a Post box

2 Select **Create Doc**

3 The document will appear. Click **Title** to alter its name

4 Click **Write something...** and begin typing

5 Click the **+ icon** and select **Photo** to use an image. Find a picture, and click **Upload New Photo**

6 You can embed images or video from the web. Select **Embed**. Copy the media's web address and paste it into the box. Click **Insert**

7 A photo can also be added to the document's header. Click the header, and choose a photo or drag an image to it

8 To let others edit the document, tick the box for **Allow other members to edit this document**

9 When you are finished, click **Publish**

Uploading a file to Groups

As long as a group's settings permit it, members are able to upload files. These can be downloaded by other members, again depending on the settings that have been applied to the group.

Beware

If you link to a file stored on Dropbox, anyone outside the Group could potentially view it.

1 Go to a group and click **More** in the Create a Post box

2 Select **Add File**

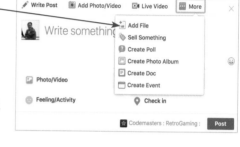

3 You will see an option to choose a file from your computer. You will also see an option to use the cloud service Dropbox. Depending on where your file is located, click **Choose File**

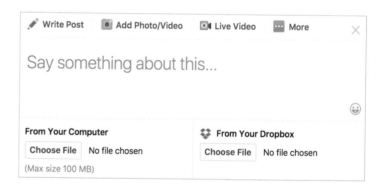

Hot tip

If you use Android, you can upload a file from your device. See page 83 for details of where the menu for this feature is located.

4 The filename will be displayed. If you have chosen the wrong file, you can repeat Step 3 and choose another file. The maximum size is 100MB

5 Explain what the file is and what you expect others to do with it

6 Click **Post**

View content on a mobile

If you want to keep a close eye on the content being uploaded to a Group, why not do so while you're on the move using the Facebook app?

1 With the Facebook app open, go to the Group you wish to view and select the **Info** button

2 You will be presented with a large number of options:

Members. Tap this to see a list of the group's members along with a separate list of admins.

Notifications. Alter how you want the notifications to appear on your mobile device.

Share group. Share details of a group on Facebook, send it as a message, or else copy the link.

Videos and Photos. These categories let you see any videos and photos that have been uploaded to the Group.

Events. Any events which have been posted appear here.

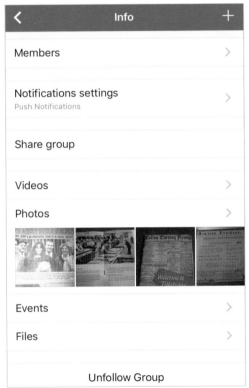

Files. If files have been uploaded to the Group, you can view a list of them by tapping Files.

Unfollowing, leaving and reporting a group via mobile

As you can see at the bottom of the screen on this page, there is also an option to unfollow a Group.

Clicking this means you remain a member but you won't receive alerts. Below this are options to leave the Group and report the Group if you find it is posting offensive material.

To report a Group via a browser on your computer, click the three-dot Menu button on the Group, and select Report Group.

Creating your own Group

Once you've familiarized yourself with how Groups work, you may decide to take the plunge and set up one of your own. You can create a Group about any subject you wish, as long as it isn't anything that could be deemed offensive.

1 Click **Groups** in Facebook's left-hand menu

2 Click the **+Create Group** button, which you'll find towards the top of the screen

+ Create Group

3 You will now see the Create New Group window. Decide on a name, and type it into the box marked **Name your group**

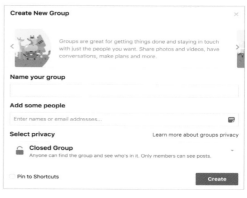

4 To set up a Group, you must enter the names or email addresses of the people that you want to invite. Click the blue Notes icon to add a personal message

5 Now you need to select how private you want your Group to be. By default, Groups are closed so while any Facebook user can find a Group, only members are able to view the posts. You can retain this setting, or else click it and choose either a Public Group, which grants anyone free access to view posts and members, or a Secret Group, which only members can find and view. Don't worry about making a mistake; you can change your mind later

6 Click **Create** when you have finished filling in the fields

7 Choose an icon that best represents your Group. You can skip this if you don't want to choose one

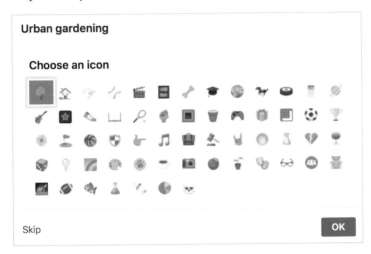

A shortcut to your Group is created. This will appear in the left-hand menu of Facebook to make it easier to visit your Group in the future.

8 Your Group will be created. It won't look much to begin with (indeed, the first entry will be the fact that you have just created it) but it is now time to start building it up by inviting more people and encouraging them to interact with the Group

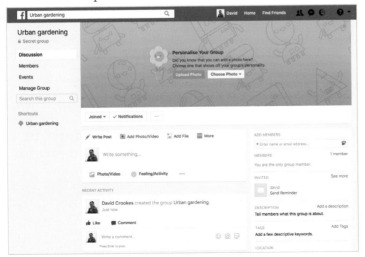

Approving new members

Even though you can add new members to your Group, you are not alone. Group members can add friends of people in the Group too. We looked at how to send invites earlier in this chapter, but here we explain how you can better control who is allowed into any Groups you create.

1 Go to your Group and click the three-dot Menu button

2 Select **Edit group settings**

3 Towards the bottom you will see a setting for **Membership Approval**

4 If you want to ultimately approve who can become a member, tick the box for **Any member can add members, but an admin or a moderator must approve them**

Membership Approval	◯ Any member can add or approve members.
	◉ Any member can add members, but an admin or a moderator must approve them.

5 Click **Save**

Approving Group posts

You can go even further and seek to approve any posts that a Group member creates. If you want to do this:

1 Click the three-dot Menu button in your Group, and select **Edit group settings** as above

2 Look for **Post Approval**

3 Tick the box for **All group posts must be approved by an admin or a moderator**

Post Approval	☑ All group posts must be approved by an admin or a moderator.

4 Click **Save**

Create extra Group admins

You'll have seen from the previous page that admins and moderators can approve members. Here we look at how you can create additional admins and moderators to work alongside yourself in looking after your Group.

1 Go to your Group and select **Members** from the left-hand menu

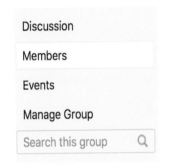

2 You will see a list of the members that are currently in your Group. Click the Settings cog, which you'll see to the right in their profile box

David Crookes
Author at In Easy Steps books for smart learning

Hot tip

If you decide you don't want a member to be an admin or moderator, follow Steps 1 and 2, and select Remove as Admin.

3 Click either **Make Admin** or **Make Moderator**

What can admins and moderators do?
Once you make someone an admin, they can:

- Make other members admins and moderators.

- Remove admins and moderators.

- Alter the settings for the Group.

Moderators cannot do any of these. Both admins and moderators can, however:

- Approve or refuse posts and membership requests.

- Remove comments, posts and people.

- Pin and unpin posts.

- Look at the support inbox.

Block and remove members

Unfortunately, as you build up a Group you may feel the need to remove a member and, to prevent them from returning, go as far as blocking them.

You may want to block somebody because:

● You don't want them to see the Group's posts.

● They are writing abusive posts.

● They are being abusive towards other members in the Group.

● Some other personal or professional reason.

You do not have to tell a person why they are being removed or blocked from your Group.

Removing and blocking a member

1 Go to your Group and select **Members** from the left-hand menu

2 Click the Settings cog in the profile box of the person you want to remove

David Crookes
Author at In Easy Steps books for smart learning

3 Select **Remove from Group**. If they want to return, they will have to ask for permission

4 Tick the box **Block Permanently** if this is a move you feel you must make. Doing this prevents them from even finding your Group when they search for it

5 Select **Confirm**

6 Anyone you block is listed on the Members page under the tag Blocked. You can select the Settings cog and opt to unblock them if you wish

Adding content via mobile

You can add content to your Group in the way we explained earlier. You can also create content via a mobile device.

1 Go to a Group in the Facebook app on your mobile device and tap the three-dot Menu button in the Create a Post box

Mobile devices are great for checking in on Groups when you're on the move.

2 If you are using Android, you will see this menu. The options will allow you to start a live video (go to Chapter 10 for more about this). You can also create a Group poll using the same structure explained on page 74 and create a Group album (which we explain more about in Chapter 10). There are options, too, for creating a Group event (which we discuss in Chapter 9),

- 📹 Start Live Video
- ▤ Create Group Poll
- 🏷 Sell Something
- 🖼 Create Group Album
- ⊞ Create Group Event
- 💬 Create Group Chat
- 🗐 Create Group File

creating Group chats (see Chapter 8) and creating Group files (for more on this, see page 76)

3 Those of you using iOS will see this menu. There are fewer options but, as with Android, you can use the Group to sell something. We look more closely at the

- 📹 Start Live Video
- ☰ Create a poll
- 📅 Create Group Event
- 🖼 Create Group Album
- $ Sell Something

principles of selling items on Facebook in Chapter 11

83

Personalizing your Group

Until you and your Group's members begin to add content, your Group will feel rather empty. But as well as producing posts, you can flesh your Group out by adding a description. You can also help others to find your Group more easily using tags and even add a location, which is perfect for flagging up the venue of a wedding or your organization's base.

Adding a description

Describing what your Group is about is a good way to encourage anybody stumbling across it to consider requesting becoming a member. You can also use it to assure anyone looking specifically for your Group that they have the correct one.

1 Go to your Group and look for the panel that lies to the right of your Group's News Feed

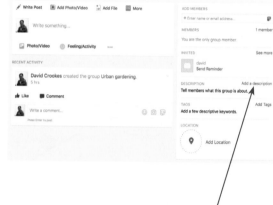

2 You will see a section labeled Description. Click the words **Add a description**

3 Write your description within the text box. Ensure it really captures the spirit of what your group is all about

4 Click **Save** when you have finished and the description will be added to your Group

Adding tags

When you add tags, think of words that best explain what your Group is about. Consider what someone searching for your Group would type into Facebook's Search bar.

1 On your group's page click **Add tags**, which you will find in the right-hand panel

2 You can write up to five tags in the text box

3 Click **Save**

Adding a location

Whether location is important to your Group (for instance, if you run a soccer team in a local park or you want to bring people in your community together for a cake sale), you can use a location tag. Anyone looking for a nearby Group will be able to find your Group more easily.

1 On your Group's page click **Add Location**, which you will find in the right-hand panel

2 Type your location in the Search bar, and either pick one of the options which appear or press Enter on your computer's keyboard

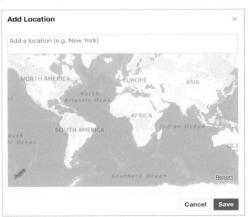

3 If it is correctly pinpointing the location you want, click **Save**

Hot tip

If you have set up a Secret Group, only current and former members will be able to view the location. Anyone can see the location of Public and Closed Groups.

85

Uploading a cover image

Nothing personalizes a Group more than a photo. You can use an image to create a striking header for your Group.

To make your cover image stand out:

● Use a clean, bold photo rather than something too busy.

● Consider using art software to create an image that incorporates the name of the Group.

● Ensure it is at least 400 pixels wide and 150 pixels tall to prevent overstretching or blurriness.

● Make it relevant to the theme of your Group.

1 If you have an image on your computer you want to use then, at the top of your Group, click **Upload Photo**

2 Search your computer for the image and select **Choose** to upload it

3 If you have previously uploaded an image to Facebook and you'd like to use that, click **Choose Photo** instead

4 Select **Choose From My Photos** if the image is stored in your own Facebook account. Or, select **Choose from Group Photos** if it has been uploaded to the Group

5 A window will appear, letting you choose an image

6 Click **Save Changes**

Pinning a post to the top

Some posts can be more significant than others. Perhaps you have written some rules that you want Group members to follow, or maybe you are looking to flag up some important information and ensure that everyone who visits the Group will see it.

You can stress the importance of a post by pinning it to the top.

1 Identify the Group post you want to pin to the top, and click the downward-facing arrow in the right-hand corner

2 Select **Pin Post** from the menu

3 If you wish to remove the pin, click the downward-facing arrow again, and select **Unpin Post**. If you don't unpin a post, it will remain forever pinned – there is no natural cut-off point

4 The post will be pinned to the top of the Group. The words Pinned Post will appear above it so that other Group members know it is of greater importance. The Group's other posts will always appear beneath this

Deleting a Group

Has your Group come to its natural end? Have you decided that you don't want to continue with it anymore? Or has it simply not proved to be as popular as you hoped? You don't actually need a reason to close and delete your Group.

1 Before you are able to close a Group, you have to formally remove each member of it. So, go to your Group and click **Members** in the menu on the left-hand side

2 Ensuring you are in the **Members** tab, go down the entire list of people, clicking the Settings cog button and selecting **Remove from Group** for each one

3 Once you have removed everybody from the group, you will be left with just yourself. Again, click the Settings cog button, but this time select **Leave Group**

4 With that action, the Group will be deleted

Keeping your options open by archiving the Group

Perhaps deleting a Group feels too drastic a move. As the admin for a group, you can archive it instead. It allows members to continue visiting, but nobody will be able to post to it or add other people. Archived groups can be brought back to life by unarchiving them at a later date.

1 On your Group page, click the three-button menu

2 Select **Archive Group**

3 When you visit the Group in the future, you'll see a message saying it has been archived, and a prominent option marked **Unarchive Group**

7 Working with Pages

Whether you run a business or are involved in any sort of organization, a Facebook Page enables you to deliver your message to anyone who wishes to follow. This chapter looks at how you can find Pages and set up one of your own.

What is a Page?

Facebook Pages are both similar yet different to Facebook Groups. While Groups are great for bringing people together to talk about a common interest, Pages are aimed at creating an official presence for a business, organization, public figure or other such body.

When you set up a Page:

● It will be public.

● It will be maintained and updated by the administrators.

● It will allow anyone to join by simply liking the Page.

● It will display your posts in your followers' News Feeds.

Pages that you create can be updated in the same way that you would update your own personal profile. By liking a Page, you will able to keep up-to-date with the latest news and, only if it is allowed by the Page administrators, communicate back.

Finding, Liking and Following a Page

1 Click the **Search** bar at the top of the screen

2 Try typing the name of an organization or public figure you want to Follow or Like

3 Look through the search results. Any Pages matching your keywords will be grouped together. Click **See All** to view all of the results

4 Click on the search entry for the Page to view what it is posting. If you like what you see, click **Like**. A post stating that you've liked a Page will appear on your News Feed. You can **Follow** a Page instead if you don't want such a post to appear in your News Feed

Hot tip

When you Like a Page, it will display Liked beneath the cover image. You can click and select Unlike This Page at any time.

Interacting with a Page

Since Pages work like personal profiles, you can interact with them in the same way. Pay attention to the options that you may see running down the left-hand column in order to make the most of a Page.

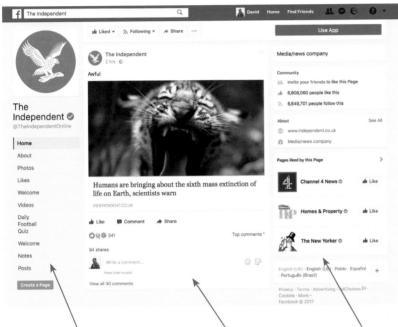

Hot tip

Visit a Page by selecting its title when you see one of its posts in your News Feed. Alternatively, select Pages from the menu to the left of your News Feed, and choose the Page you want.

The Menu. Use this column to navigate around the Page. It may highlight specific types of content such as photos or videos, polls, and more.

News Feed. This column lists all of the posts created by the Page's administrators. Keep scrolling to see more of them.

Information. This column includes information about the Page, with links and the number of people liking and following it.

Writing a comment

1. To react with an emoji, select **Like** and choose a thumbs-up, heart, or one of the four emotional faces

2. Click **Share** if you wish to share the Page with your friends or within your own Group or Page

3. Click the **Comment** box to write a message

Hot tip

Some Pages will let you create new posts. If so, you will see a Create a Post box towards the top of the Page. Click to write something, or to post a photo or video.

Creating your own Page

Anyone can create their own Page, but you have to bear a few things in mind.

- If you are creating a Page about a corporate entity or a brand such as a soccer club, movie, musician, newspaper, political party or charity, you must be in an official position to be able to do so. Otherwise, look to set up a Group instead.

- Anybody will be able to view the posts that you create, and you will not be given a say in who can Like or Follow you before they do so, although you can ban people later.

- Be sure that you have the time to update the Page and moderate it. Rarely-updated Pages can be annoying for those who Like or Follow them. Any posts made by members won't be flagged up in the News Feeds of other members, so you can't rely on them to keep your Page looking active.

Getting started

1 Click **Pages** in the left-hand Menu bar

2 Select **Create Page** at the top of the screen

3 Choose the kind of Page you wish to create. There are six choices: Local business or place; Company, Organization or Institution; Brand or product; Artist, Band or Public Figure; Entertainment; and Cause or Community

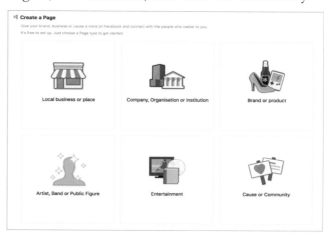

4 When you click a category, you will be asked to fill in a few fields. For a local business or place, you will input a business or place name, address and phone number. For everything else, you need to select a category and input a name. The only exception is for a cause or community, where a name alone is all that's required

There are certain restrictions on the names you can use. You can't violate copyright, be abusive, use the word Facebook or symbols, for instance. You'll be told if a name is not permitted.

5 Once you have completed the required fields in the box, click **Get Started**. You will then be taken to your fledgling Page, which you can now begin to describe, build up with content, and promote

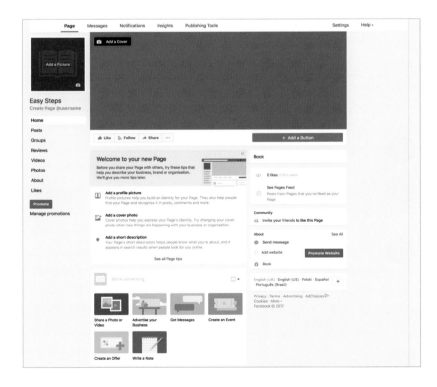

Creating a Page username

A great way to personalize your Page and make it easier for others to find is to create a unique username. This will then allow you to produce a web address that you can share with other people.

1 Select **Create Page @username**, which you can find under the section for a profile image to the left of the Facebook interface

Easy Steps
Create Page @username

2 Enter the username you wish to use in the box marked Username

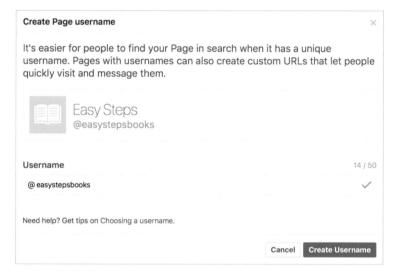

3 Click **Create Username**

4 Facebook will check whether the username is available and, it if is, you will be able to make use of it

5 If you ever need to change the username, then you can click **About** in the left-hand menu and, in the General section at the top, select **Edit** next to the entry for Username. Again, the username will need to be available in order for you to be able to make use of it

6 Tell others about your username so they can use it

Building up a great Page

There are some basic elements involved in any Page:

- A profile picture

- A cover photo

- A short description explaining what the Page is about

Adding a profile image

1 In the profile image box, click **Add a Picture**

2 Select either **Take Photo** or **Upload Photo**

3 If taking a fresh photo, grant Facebook access to your camera and mic. Click **Take Photo** when you are ready

4 If you're uploading a photo, find the image on your computer, and use the Facebook tool to position it and crop. Click **Save**. See more about images in Chapter 10

Adding a cover photo

1 Click **Add a Cover**, which you will see in the main box at the top of the screen

2 Select **Upload Photo** and browse for an image on your computer. Click **Save**

Adding a description

1 Click **About** in the left-hand menu of your Page

2 Look for **About** under More Info, and click **Edit**

3 Write your description, and click **Save**

Hot tip

Cover images must be at least 400 pixels wide and 150 pixels tall.

Information and images are not set in stone.

Adding essential information

As well as a short description, it is a good idea to add contact information and links to any associated websites, as well as more details about the product, brand, company or organization that you are creating the Page for. You will find the options for these on the About screen.

1 Click **About** in the left-hand menu

2 You'll see lots of options, such as the ability to enter a phone number, email address or product details. Look at each entry and decide if you want to add the required information. Click **Edit** to add or change the details

3 The information you will be asked to provide will be different for each genre of Page. If you are promoting a book, for instance, you could add details about its release date, publisher and ISBN. Businesses can add opening hours, while restaurants can upload a photo or PDF menu

Creating a post on your Page

Writing a post for your Page is slightly different to writing one for your Profile. There are a few extra options to consider before you decide to publish.

Creating a basic post

1 Click the **Create a Post** box on your Page and write something in the box

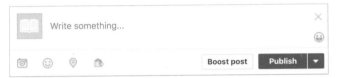

2 To add a photo or video, click the **Camera** icon to the far left and look for the file on your computer. Press Choose when you have found and selected it

3 Click the smiley-face icon to the right of the Camera to add an **Emoji**, or **Check in** by clicking the Pin icon

4 Your posts can also include emojis (click the open-mouthed face to do this). When ready, click **Publish**

Saving a draft

If you want to come back to a post later without sending it immediately, you can save a draft.

1 Follow Steps 1 to 3 above but instead of clicking Publish, select the downward arrow

2 Click **Save Draft**

3 A Draft box will appear beneath the Create a Post box. Click **See Draft** to resume

4 Select the post from the list and either click **Edit**, or select the downward arrow and click **Publish**

Scheduling your posts

Facebook lets you schedule your posts before you publish them.

1 Instead of clicking Publish as in Step 4 on page 97, click the downward arrow instead and select **Schedule**

2 Tick the box next to **Publication** and click the calendar to create a date. Input a time, and change the zone if need be

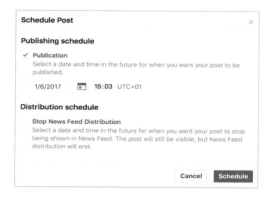

3 You can also tick the box next to **Stop News Feed Distribution** if you want to create a date when the post will stop being shown in the News Feed

4 When you're ready, click **Schedule**

Backdating your post

You can also date your posts so they appear to have been written in the past.

1 Follows Steps 1 to 3 on page 97 and click the downward arrow next to Publish

2 Select **Backdate**

3 Select a year, month and day. You can also choose if you want to hide the post from your News Feed

4 Click **Backdate**

Tag products to your posts

When you are creating a post, you will see an icon that looks like a bag with a price tag. Clicking this allows you to tag products in your post. Here is how it works.

1 Click the **Create a Post** box on your Page

2 Click the **Tag Products** icon

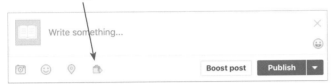

3 Type the name of a product or its ID, and press Enter on your keyboard

4 The first time you do this for a particular item, you'll be asked to fill in details about it. In the window that appears, add a photo, fill in the product's name, add a price (moving the slider to blue if it is on sale and inputting a sale price), and write a description

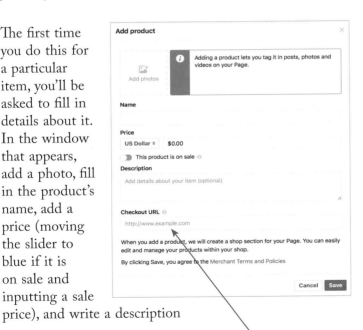

5 Add a website address to the box marked **Checkout URL**. Anyone wanting to buy the product will be sent to the web page

6 Click **Save**

Create content-rich posts

As well as writing text-based posts, you can click a series of icons at the top of your Page's Timeline to:

- Share a Photo or Video

- Get Messages

- Create an Event or Offer

- Write a Note or Advertise your Business

Sharing a Photo or Video

1 Click **Share a Photo or Video**

2 If you choose to upload a photo or video or create a photo album, select the images you want to use from your computer, click **Choose**, create Tags if need be, and click **Publish**

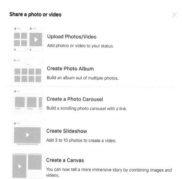

3 If you select to produce a scrolling photo carousel, create a slideshow or combine images and video into a canvas, then turn to Chapter 10 for more details

Getting messages

You can create an image-based post, which allows members to click Chat and send you a message via Messenger.

1 Click **Get Messages**

2 Select the option **Click to select an image** and choose one from your computer

3 Click **Publish**

Creating an event

By clicking Create an Event, you are able to set up a public event. We cover events in great detail in Chapter 9. Note that you can add a direct link to the ticketing website you are using, and you can also add other Pages as your co-host.

Creating an offer

You are able to upload an offer and a promo code to your page if you are selling an item.

1   Click **Create an Offer**

2   Create an expiry date and time

3   Upload an image by clicking **Add Photo**. A coupon you have created in an art package will work well here

4   Select where people can redeem the offer, whether in a store or online

5   You can click **Add Promo Code** and input a code you wish to use for your offer

6   Click **Publish**

Writing a note

Select Write a Note and turn to page 78 to find out more about how to create one.

Advertising your business

You can invite friends to share your Page and you can also advertise with Facebook. Select Advertise your Business to see the available options.

Hot tip

If you use the Call Now button, users can tap it and immediately phone your organization.

Adding a button to a Page

If you want members to be able to quickly perform certain actions such as learn more about your Page, get in touch, download a game, make a purchase or donate money, you can add a button.

1 Click **+ Add a Button** at the top of the Page

+ Add a Button

2 Select the kind of button you wish to use from the menu (for example, **Get in Touch**)

3 Select an option from the submenu (for example, **Call Now**, **Contact Us**, **Sign Up** or **Send Email**)

4 Fill in the required information (for example, if you have selected Call Now, input a phone number, or if you've chosen Send Email, input an email address)

5 Click **Add Button**

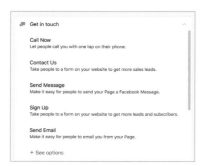

Using Partner apps and services

Play around with Facebook's buttons to start with, but do check out the buttons provided by partner apps and services once you become confident about using them.

If you run a café or restaurant, for instance, you may want to explore using the **delivery.com** button, which will let you add an ordering facility.

Each button will contain instructions for setting them up.

Get an insight into your Page

Facebook has a set of tools which lets you monitor your Page and learn how it is being used.

1 Click **Insights** at the top of your Page

2 Select an option from the left-hand menu:

- **Overview**: See a seven-day summary that notes data such as the number of Page views, post engagements, reach, Page likes, actions and videos.

- **Promotions**: If you have created an ad to promote your Page, the activity will appear here.

- **Likes**: Get a snapshot of how many likes your Page has had and where they are coming from.

- **Reach**: A chance to work out what may have caused a fall in the number of Shares, Comments and Likes.

- **Page views**: See where visitors to your Page are looking when they browse and where they are being directed from.

- **Actions on Page**: See what people are doing when they visit your Page.

- **Posts**: Figure how effective your posts are in terms of getting others to respond to them.

- **Events**: See events that you are hosting and those coming up.

- **Videos**: Select a date range and see how people are engaging with your video content, complete with viewership figures.

- **Messages**: View a snapshot of the conversations that are being had.

3 You can export the data by clicking Overview and selecting **Export Data**, selecting the date range and file format you want the record to be in

Insights is a valuable tool for working out how effective your Page is to Facebook users.

Overview
Promotions
Likes
Reach
Page views
Actions on Page
Posts
Events
Videos
Messages

Moderating your Pages

Unfortunately, a Page is not always going to run as smoothly as you may like. From time to time, someone may leave a comment that you will want to remove while others may misbehave, forcing you to consider banning them.

Go through your Settings
You can make life easier by taking some time to look through your Page's settings.

Hot tip

Hide comments from a post by selecting the downward arrow when you hover over it and selecting Hide Comments. Do it again and select Delete if you want to remove it.

1 Click **Settings** at the top of the Page

2 Click the categories to the left to view more and more Settings. Some you may want to pay particular attention to in the General tab are:

- **Visitor posts**: Decide if anyone should be able to publish to a Page or add photos and videos.

- **Profanity filter**: Activate this, and words deemed offensive by Facebook will be blocked.

- **Page moderation**: Add your own words to block.

- **Messages**: Prevent people from contacting your Page privately if it is causing a problem.

3 Click **Save Changes**

Banning people from your Page

1 Click **Settings** at the top of the Page

2 Select **People and other Pages**

3 Find the person you want to ban, and click the Cog icon

4 Select **Ban From Page**

5 Click **Confirm**

8 Using Facebook Messenger

There will be moments when you just want to have a private conversation with a friend or group of people. This chapter shows how you can use Messenger to send text, video or photo messages; play games; and even make voice and video calls to your friends for free.

What is Messenger?

Although you may be used to texting your friends, family members, colleagues and others, there are many alternatives to the standard text messaging services built into today's phones.

Referred to as instant messaging apps, they have become hugely popular. Services such as WhatsApp and Google Hangouts typically allow you to use the internet to send messages, images and documents, and make voice and video calls.

Yet one service – Facebook Messenger – has been growing at a blistering rate. Indeed, with more than 1.2 billion users, it is now one of the world's largest instant messaging apps and a social network in its own right.

It is not bad-going for a service which only began in 2014, when Facebook made the decision to split the ability to message people using the Facebook app into a separate Messenger application. Available for Android, iOS and Windows Phone, as well as on your computer desktop via an internet browser, it lets you:

- **Text chat without needing a cellphone number**. You only need to be connected with the person you wish to contact.

- **Make voice and video calls**. Face-to-face conversations are easy, and you are even able to send voice recordings.

- **Set up group chats**. If you want to share information or have a conversation with more than one person, you can.

- **Take and send photos and videos**. Sharing media is simple, and it you can snap images and record videos from within the Messenger app.

- **Have lots of fun**. Aside from being able to use stickers and experiment with a host of chatbots (computer programs which simulate human conversations), you can challenge your Messenger contacts to play lots of different games.

What's more, you can get set up without needing to create a new account. Simply use your Facebook username and password.

Installing Messenger

Since Messenger is a separate app, you will need to install it alongside Facebook on your phone or tablet.

Installing on Android

You can also access Messenger on the web at **messenger.com**

1 Tap the Play Store icon on your Android Home screen

2 Search for **Messenger** using the Search bar at the top of the screen

3 Select the entry which bears the logo

4 Tap **Install**

Installing on iOS

1 Tap the App Store icon on your iOS Home screen

2 Tap the Search icon at the bottom of the screen, and type **Messenger** in the Search bar which appears

3 Look for Messenger in the search results list, and tap **Get** when you see it

4 Tap **Install**

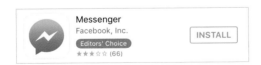

Setting up Messenger

There are two ways of opening Messenger on your smartphone or tablet device:

- **Tap the app icon.** You will find this on the Home screen of your device.

- **Tap the Messenger icon in Facebook**. You will find this in the top right-hand corner of the Facebook app.

From there, you will be taken through some initial steps aimed at setting up the Messenger app.

Getting started

1 Select whether or not you already have a Facebook account. We're assuming that you do since you have got this far into the book, so tap **I have a Facebook account**. It is worth bearing in mind that if

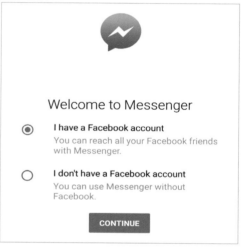

Welcome to Messenger

◉ I have a Facebook account
You can reach all your Facebook friends with Messenger.

○ I don't have a Facebook account
You can use Messenger without Facebook.

CONTINUE

you ever decide not to use Facebook in the future, you can still use Messenger without it

2 Enter the email or phone number that you used when signing up to Facebook, and type in your password in order to log in

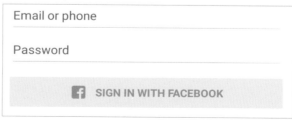

Email or phone

Password

f SIGN IN WITH FACEBOOK

Allowing others to reach you

To make the most of Messenger, you may want to widen the number of people you can contact through it. Messenger will continue to take you through this setup process.

1 You should see a screen entitled **Text anyone in your phone**. This is Messenger's way of asking to access your contacts and it will use the information it finds to see how many of your friends, colleagues, relatives and others are also using Messenger

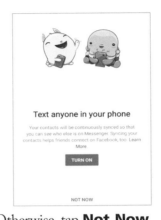

2 Decide whether or not you want Messenger to do this. If you do, simply tap the button **Turn On**. Otherwise, tap **Not Now**

3 If you do decline the offer and change your mind, don't worry: you can do it later. Tap your profile image at the top of the Messenger screen, select People and turn on Sync Contacts

Adding your phone number

If you do not have a phone number associated with your Facebook account, Messenger will ask you to input it (tap **Not Now** if you do not want to do this).

1 Tap the country shown on the screen and change it to the territory your number is associated with

2 Enter your phone number

3 Tap **OK**

4 If you decline to do this right now, you can do it later. Tap your profile image at the top of the Messenger screen, select Phone and enter it from there

Understanding the interface

Facebook Messenger packs a lot of information and many sections onto its main screen. But take a small amount of time to familiarize yourself, and you'll soon feel comfortable with it.

Looking at the icons

To get this Messenger screen in Android, we avoided syncing any contacts. But the uncluttered view gives us a great opportunity to work out the basics of the Messenger interface and examine what each of the icons do.

Search. Look for people and Groups by tapping the Search bar and typing a search term.

Your Profile. Tapping this icon gives you access to your Messenger settings.

Write a message. When you are ready to type and send a message, select this icon.

People. Search for people, see message requests, invite others, check who is active and view which of your contacts have Messenger already.

Home. This takes you back to the main screen.

Phone. Make a voice or video call.

Camera. Take a photo or record a video.

Groups. Any Groups you are involved with will be listed when you click this icon.

Q Search for people and groups

Get started

Tap 🖃 to send a message.

Tap ☰ to add your contacts.

The screens for iOS and Windows Phone may differ in terms of the arrangement of these functions, but the icons are similar.

...cont'd

Familiarizing yourself with Messenger's layout

We look at the iOS screen here. You will see the icon for sending a message is top right and the profile icon is top left.

You will also see that Messenger splits itself into sections (note: we have deliberately obscured the profile images in this shot).

Chats.
Your recent conversations appear here. Contacts that also use Messenger have a blue lightning bolt embedded within their profile image. Others have a gray Facebook badge instead.

New contacts.
When you connect with someone new, this information is prominently flagged.

Messenger Day.
The Messenger Day feature is a photo feed which lets you curate related photos and videos in one place. They will disappear after 24 hours.

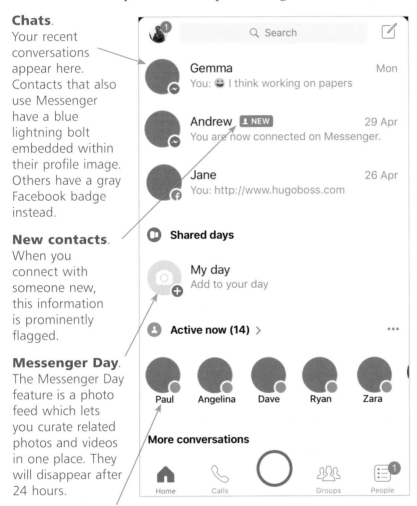

Active contacts. If your contacts are currently using Messenger, then they will appear here.

More conversations. Keep scrolling to see more of your chats. If you have lots of chats, they will keep loading on to the screen until you reach the end. You are also allowed to have as many chat threads as you like, so don't worry about connecting with others and enjoying your many conversations.

Write and send a message

One of the first things you will want to do when you start using Messenger is write and send somebody a message. There are two key ways of doing this:

- Start a new conversation with somebody

- Respond to an established thread

Starting a new conversation

1 From the **Home** tab, tap on the **Write Message** icon

2 Choose the person you wish to chat with. You can add multiple names if you wish to hold a conversation with more than one person

Responding to an established thread

1 Tap the **Home** tab

2 Scroll down the list of conversations, and tap the message you want to respond to

Creating the message

After establishing who you want to send your message to, you are now ready to create it.

1 Look towards the bottom of the screen. You will see a box containing the letters Aa. Tap the **Text Box** to bring the keyboard on to the screen

2 Start typing your message using the keyboard

3 When you have finished, tap the Send button

Sending stickers and emoji

They say a picture paints a thousand words, and that is also true when you're creating messages in Messenger. You can send:

- **Stickers**. Fun illustrated pictures and animations.

- **GIFs**. Hilarious moving images with no sound.

- **Emoji**. Digital images used to express ideas and emotion.

Want even more choice? When selecting Stickers, tap the **+** icon and you can access the Sticker Store for extra goodies.

1 Tap the smiley face in the **Text Box**

2 Select either the **Stickers**, **GIFs** or **Emoji** tab

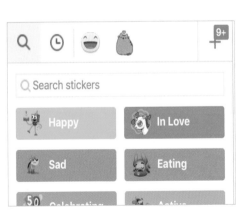

3 After selecting **Stickers** or **Emoji**, you can look through the images. Tap one you would like to use, and it will appear in the Text Box

4 To help narrow your search and prevent endless scrolling, Messenger groups Stickers and Emoji together. Click the **Categories** to help narrow your search

5 If you select **GIFs**, you can scroll through a selection that appears in the center of the screen. You can also try typing various search terms if you wish to look for something more specific. GIFs cover a large range of subject matters

Sending a photo or video

You can attach photos and videos to your messages. They can be:

- Photos or videos stored on your device

- Photos or videos taken fresh using the camera from within the Messenger app

Sending a previously-saved photograph or video

1 There are a set of icons to the left of the Text Box.
If you cannot see them, tap the arrow

2 Tap the Photograph icon

3 A selection of images will appear at the bottom of the
screen. Scroll through them, and tap the
one you want to send to your contact. If you
want to see your photos displayed on a full
screen for easier browsing, tap the icon in
the bottom-left corner

4 You will have a
choice to **Edit**
or **Send** the
image – they
will appear as
written words
in iOS and as
symbols in Android

5 We will look at editing images in greater depth in
Chapter 10 but, for now, tapping **Send** will create a
message using your photo and send it on its way

6 When a blue tick appears next to the image in the
conversation thread, you will know it has been successfully
delivered to your contact

...cont'd

Sending a new photograph taken using the camera

1 To take a very quick snap, press and hold the **Photo** icon to the left of the Text Box

2 A pop-up window will appear. Line up your shot and let go to automatically send it. To delete the image before sending, drag it up the screen until it turns red

3 For a more composed shot, simply tap the **Camera** icon to the left of the Text Box

4 This will take you to Facebook's in-app camera feature (which we will cover in more depth in Chapter 10). Use the **Shutter** button to take a photo

5 If you are pleased with the image, tap the right-facing arrow to send it to your contact

Sending a new video recorded using the camera

1 If you want to send a video clip, press and hold the **Camera** icon rather than simply tapping it

2 A short video will record. You will see how much time is left by viewing the bar within the recording window

3 Drag the video up the screen during the recording to delete it

4 When the recording ends, it will be sent as a message

Send a voice message

Whether your fingers are tired or you feel something is just better explained verbally, Messenger will allow you to record and send a voice message.

1 Tap and hold the **Microphone** icon to the left of the Text Box when you are about to create a message

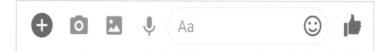

2 **Speak** to your device hands-free, and the microphone will pick up and record what you are saying

3 If you decide to abandon the message, just drag it up the screen to cancel

4 Otherwise, when you let go, the recording will end

5 It will be instantly placed into a message and sent

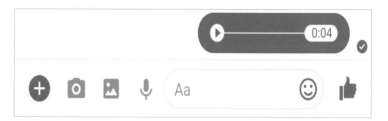

Listening to a recorded voice message

1 When the message is received (and the same applies when you are sent such a message too), you can listen back by tapping the Play button within the voice message box that appears in the conversation thread

2 You can tap again to pause it at any point

Play some fun games

Fancy challenging your friends to a game of Pac-Man or Space Invaders? How about Words With Friends or Daily Sudoku? Messenger's Instant Games platform has dozens of titles, and you can not only go head-to-head with others but also compete for a place on leaderboards and take part in tournaments, depending on the game you are enjoying.

Lots of games developers are involved in creating titles for Messenger, so keep checking back to see what is being added.

1 Tap a conversation thread in Messenger, or tap the **Compose Message** icon and choose a contact

2 Tap the **+** icon to the left of the Text Box

3 Select **Games**

4 Look down the list of games. The latest releases are in the top section, while any games you choose will appear underneath in a section marked Played recently. More games appear as you scroll down

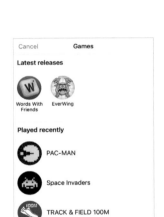

5 Tap a game you like the look of, and it will load. By tapping **Play Now** you can challenge your contact to beat your score

6 The controls should appear on the screen, showing you how to play

7 Your score appears when the game ends

8 Tap **Play Again** if you would like to have another attempt at the game

Hot tip

If you receive a map, tap the pin and you'll be able to open it in a map app and get directions.

Sharing your location

While we have some concerns about sharing your location with a wide number of people on Facebook, allowing specific contacts to know your whereabouts can be useful, especially if you are arranging to meet or if you need to help someone find your current location.

1 Tap a conversation thread, or tap the **Write Message** icon and choose a contact

2 Tap the **+** icon to the left of the Text Box

3 Select **Location**

4 You must allow Messenger to access the location of your device. (In Android, select **Allow** and in iOS go to the **Settings** app and navigate to Privacy > Location Services. Scroll down and tap Messenger, then select either While Using the App or Always)

5 A map will appear on the screen, pinpointing your current location. You can also search for other locations

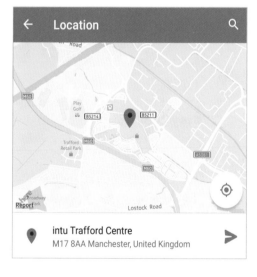

6 When you have found a location, tap **Send** in iOS or tap the Send icon in Android

7 The location will be sent. The recipient can than click the map to see the location in greater detail

Have a secret conversation

By default, your conversations are not fully encrypted. That means they could be potentially intercepted and read, even though the chances of someone doing that is small. If this worries you, there is a way of holding a conversation using end-to-end encryption. By activating it, no-one will be able to read your messages, and that includes Facebook itself.

Using iOS

1 Tap the **Write Message** icon

2 Tap **Secret** in the top right-hand corner

3 Select who you wish to message

4 Tap **Start Secret Conservation** at the bottom of the screen

5 Begin writing your message as usual

Using Android

1 Choose somebody to start a conversation with

2 Tap the Info icon in the top-right corner

3 Tap **Go to Secret Conservation** and begin writing your message

Go to Secret Conversation

4 Your conversation will have end-to-end encryption

Beware

Nothing would stop the recipient of your messages (or indeed, yourself) from taking a screenshot of your secret conversation and sharing that with others.

Beware

Messenger will make you aware that new secret conversations will only be available on the device you are using. That means the conversation won't appear in Messenger apps on other platforms.

Hot tip

Use the Timer button in the Text Box to set how long your message should appear for.

If someone is not on the internet, you may not be able to have a conversation with them.

Make phone and video calls

You may well have heard of services such as Skype, FaceTime and Google Hangouts, which allow you to make calls using the internet. Messenger has its own such feature. You can make top-quality calls across the globe for free and without eating into the minutes of your phone's data plan. You can also have face-to-face video chats, which are also free as long as you're using Wi-Fi.

Making a phone call to one person

1 Tap the **Calls** button, which you will find at the bottom of your device's screen

2 Look down your list of contacts or use the Search bar to look for someone manually

3 When you find someone you wish to contact, tap the **Calls** button next to their name

Making a phone call to a group

1 Tap on the **Calls** button at the bottom of the screen

2 Tap the **Groups** button next to New Call in iOS or select **Start Group Call** in Android

> Q Search for people and groups
>
> ⠿ Start Group Call

3 Go down the list, and tap the people you wish to have a group conversation with

4 Tap the **Calls** button to begin the conversation

Making a video call to one person

1 Tap the **Calls** button

2 Scroll down the list of contacts or search manually for their name

3 Select the **Video** button next to their name

Beware

If you are not connected to Wi-Fi, you may be charged for any data you use when making calls.

Making a phone call to a group

1 Tap the **Calls** button

2 Tap the **Groups** button in iOS or select **Start Group Call** in Android

3 In the list, tap all of the people you wish to hold a face-to-face video chat with

4 Tap the **Video** button to connect with each of them, and begin chatting away

Hot tip

Control who can see your My Day by tapping your profile image in Messenger and tapping My Day from the options.

Using Messenger Day

If you would like to use Messenger to share your photos and videos as they happen, you can do so using Messenger Day. It allows you to create a story, with everything you share with your contacts on Messenger disappearing after 24 hours.

1 Tap the **Home** button and tap the **Circle** button that appears at the bottom of the screen

2 Tap the **Circle** button on the next screen to take a photo, or hold to record a video

3 You can add effects such as overlaid graphics. Scroll through the images you will see above the Circle button. Tap the Palette button to add text or to draw something

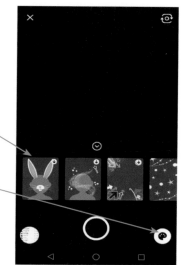

4 Tap the arrow

5 Select My Day. It will remain within My Day for 24 hours and you will be able to see who views it

6 Tap the Send arrow ➤

7 Your photo/video will now be viewable on your My Day

9 Create and join events

Don't fear missing out. This chapter looks at how you can receive and manage invites to events. It also shows you how to create events, send invitations and generate some publicity.

Receiving invites to events

Millions of events take place across the world each and every year. There are birthdays to celebrate, weddings to attend and numerous graduations, bachelor and bachelorette parties, launches, openings, leaving drinks, house-warming gatherings, and so much more.

Facebook allows you to create and receive invitations to events. You can then respond to the invitation, indicating whether or not you are likely to attend. Doing so helps events planner, work out how many people they need to cater for. Invites can also help spread the word about a public event.

Viewing and responding to an invite

Beware

When you indicate that you are interested in an event or are going, the information will be posted to your Timeline.

1 When you are invited to an event, you will receive a notification. You can also view the events you are invited to by clicking on the Events tab in the left-hand menu of the Facebook website, or by tapping the Menu button in the Facebook app and selecting Events

Beware

Looked at a private invite? The event creator and the guests who are going will know you have viewed it.

2 Any events that you have been invited to will appear at the top of the screen. Each invitation will show you who has sent the invite. Click on the event to see more details about it. You will be able to see how many other people have stated they are going

London Gaming Market - Sunday 23rd Jul...
Sunday, July 23 at 11 AM
Royal National Hotel
Andy invited you to this public event

| Interested | Going | Ignore |

3 If the event is public, you will have three options. You can indicate that you are **Interested** or you can state that you are **Going**. If you would prefer not to choose either, you can also simply select **Ignore**

4 If the event is private, the options are different. You will be asked to state whether you are **Going**, considering going (so **Maybe**) or **Can't Go**

Hot tip

You can change your mind about an event by revisiting it and selecting a different response.

Exploring other events

You don't have to be invited to an event to be able to see what's going on. Facebook will flag up any events taking place near to your location and you will also be able to see events that are proving to be popular among your friends. Facebook will also make suggestions.

1 Click the Events tab in the left-hand menu of the Facebook website, or open the Facebook app, tap the Menu button and select Events

2 Below the invites, you will see a section of events near your current location. Click **Today** or **This weekend**

3 You will see more options in the left-hand menu, including **Next Week** and **Choose a date**. Select **Interested** if you fancy attending any of the events

4 Going back to the main Events page, you will see another section marked **Popular with Friends**. These include events that your friends are interested in. You can select **Interested** or **Going** on any of these

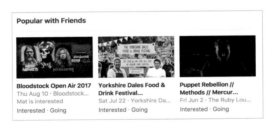

Popular with Friends

Bloodstock Open Air 2017
Thu Aug 10 · Bloodstock...
Mat is interested
Interested · Going

Yorkshire Dales Food &
Drink Festival...
Sat Jul 22 · Yorkshire Da...
Interested · Going

Puppet Rebellion //
Methods // Mercur...
Fri Jun 2 · The Ruby Lou...
Interested · Going

5 Another section marked **Suggested for You** picks out events that Facebook thinks you will enjoy. Express an interest

6 Both the app and the website have categories that help filter the events you will see. Scroll to the bottom of the app and website screens to select them

Want to see past events? On the main Events page, select Past in the left-hand menu.

Clicking Calendar in the left-hand menu lets you see events by date.

Facebook users in the US can download an events app for iOS and Android. Look for "Events from Facebook" in the App Store or Google Play.

See the events a friend is already attending by going to their profile, clicking **More** underneath their cover image, and selecting Events (if they have not hidden this section).

Sharing an event

If you want others to join in the fun of a public event, you can share it. At the same time, you are able to limit the number of people who you share it with.

1 Find an event that interests you and select it. It may be an event that you are already attending or one you are simply considering: sharing can help encourage others to go along with you

2 Beneath the profile header on both the Facebook website and the Facebook app for iOS is a **Share** button. Click it. If you are using Android, you will find the share option within the three-dot menu on the event page

3 Choose how you want to share it. You can:

- **Invite Friends**. Select this and you will see a list of friends. Tap their names and select **Invite** or **Send Invites**.

- **Share in your News Feed**. The event will be turned into a link that you can write something about before selecting **Post**.

- **Share in Messenger**. Send it as a direct, private message to friends using Facebook Messenger.

4 Sharing an event using a mobile? Selecting **More Options** lets you send the event as a link via email or a different messaging service. You can also copy the link or share it on alternative social networks, including Twitter

Controlling event invites

You may be attending an event that you don't want others to know about. Perhaps you've been invited but, by expressing you are interested, you risk upsetting those who haven't been asked. Or maybe you just don't want to promote exactly where you are going to be at a certain point in time in the future.

Hiding your interest in an event

1 To prevent others from knowing that you are interested in attending an event, you can save it instead. Click the three-dot menu on the page for the event

2 Click or tap **Save**

Blocking somebody from sending you invites

1 For whatever reason, you may not want to receive an invite from a specific person. If this is the case, click the downward-facing arrow in the top-right of Facebook

2 Select **Settings**

3 Select **Blocking** from the left-hand menu

> Privacy
> Timeline and Tagging
> Blocking
> Language

4 Look down the list for **Block event invites** and type in the names of a friend

Block event invites Once you block event invites from someone, you'll automatically ignore future event requests from that friend.

Block invites from Type the name of a friend...

5 Any future event requests from that person will be automatically ignored

Receiving event notifications

Once you have decided you would like to attend an event, you can enjoy receiving notifications about it. You should be kept up-to-date with any changes or discover more about what is going to take place. Notifications often act as a nice reminder about a forthcoming event and they can heighten the levels of excitement you feel about attending.

Event notifications appear within the Notifications section of Facebook, and you can access them by selecting the Globe icon on the website and app.

But what if you want the notifications to stop?

Control the event notifications

1 Visit the page of the event that you have expressed a positive interest in attending

2 Select the three-dot Menu icon or tap the More button on the app

3 Click or tap **Notification Settings**

4 Choose one of the following four options:

- **All notifications**. Selecting this ensures you receive every notification.

- **Highlights**. You will only see the most important information from the organizers and friends.

- **Host updates only**. Only the information posted by the organizers will be flagged up.

- **Off**. You won't receive any more notifications about the event.

5 Click Done on the website or tap the Back button in the mobile app

Viewing upcoming birthdays

Facebook will notify you of a friend's birthday as long as they have included the date in their profile. You'll be told ahead of time and on the day. There is a special section within events too.

1   Keep an eye on your notifications, where information about birthdays are flagged up. You are encouraged to send good thoughts

> It's **Brendan**'s birthday today. Send him good thoughts!
> 1 May at 08:27

2   To see other birthdays, click Events in the left-hand menu. On the Events page, select **Birthdays**

3   Recent birthdays are shown first, together with any action you took such as writing a message on their Timeline to wish them well. Upcoming birthdays are listed next

4   You can also click on the Calendar in the left-hand menu and see birthdays plotted by date. Hover over one of the profile images on the calendar to see more details

Exporting your friends' birthdays

If you want to plot your friends' birthdays in Google Calendar, Microsoft Outlook or Apple Calendar, you can export the information from Facebook. You can also do this with any event.

1   Click Events in the left-hand menu and look over to the third column of the Events page. You will see this box

> You can add your events to Microsoft Outlook, Google Calendar or Apple Calendar. Once you add them, they'll stay updated. **Learn More.**
> Upcoming Events
> Birthdays

2   Select either **Birthdays** or **Upcoming Events**, depending on the kind of events you want to export

3   You'll then be given the option to open it within a calendar program

Creating an event

If you are hosting an event, whether private or public, you too can use Facebook not only to promote it, but also to invite people along.

Getting started

1 Go to the Events page via the left-hand menu in Facebook, and click **+Create Event**. If you are using the app, go to the Events section and tap **Create** in iOS or the blue **+** icon at the bottom of the screen in Android

2 Choose between a private or public event. In the app, tap Private Event at the top of the screen to toggle between Private and Public

✉ **Create Private Event**
Only invited guests will see your event. You can choose to let guests invite friends

🌐 **Create Public Event**
Anyone will be able to see your event and search for it, even if you're not friends

130

Creating a private event using the website

Once you create a private event you are unable to switch back to a public one, so bear that in mind right from the start. Facebook warns you in the Event setup window.

Choose a Theme. Click this button to include a visual themes. Choose images for parties; birthdays; food and drink; family; holiday; travel; recreation; and seasons.

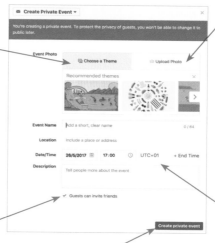

Upload Photo. You can also choose a photo or graphic taken or created yourself.

Input details. Fill in the event name, location of your event, the start time (click End Time to include an end time too) and a description.

Invitations. If you want guests to be able to invite friends to your event, make sure you tick the box at the bottom.

Create private event. When you've finished entering the details, click this button. Your event page will be created. You will then be ready to promote the event and send invites.

Creating a public event using the website

The Public Event setup window is slightly different.

Add Event Photo. There are no pre-made themes for public events. Instead, you have to add your own image. It suggests this be 1920 x 1080 pixels.

Event info. You still need to input an event name and location, but as well as a start time you have to add an end time too. It's not optional this time.

Details. The description is even more important here because you'll want to appeal to the public. You also need to add some keywords that will be useful when people search for your event.

Options. Decide whether posts have to be approved or whether you would rather respond only if others complain about a post.

Once you have decided on a private or public event, you can't change your mind once the event has been created.

Finishing off the creation of your public event

1 You are able to save the draft of your Event setup and finish off later if you wish by clicking **Save Draft**

2 You can also schedule when you want the event to appear by clicking the downward arrow next to Create, selecting **Schedule**, and inputting the time and date

3 Otherwise, click **Create**

Inviting people by text or email, and none of your friends are listed? See page 21 for details of how to import contacts.

132

You can "only" personally invite 500 people to your event. By allowing friends attending the event to also invite people, you can get around this restriction if need be.

Sending event invitations

To make people aware of a private event, you will need to invite your friends to it. Friends do not have to be on Facebook to be invited. You can invite people by email and text.

1 On the page for your event, click **Invite**

2 Select **Choose Friends**

3 Go down the list of friends and choose people to invite

4 If you want to invite people who are not on Facebook, click Invite as in Step 1 but select **Invite by text or email**

5 Again, choose the friends you wish to invite. When you are done, click **Send Invitations**

Inviting friends on a mobile device

1 Open the page for your event in the app and, at the bottom of the screen, click **Invite Friends**

2 Select the people you want to invite. Toggle the slider at the bottom of the screen if you want to add a note with Messenger (*only if using iOS at the time of this book's publication*). Click **Invite** when you are finished

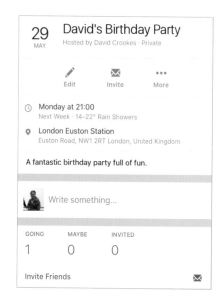

Managing your event

Once you have created your event, you will want to keep a close eye on who is responding to it.

1 Go to the page for your event

2 If your event is private, click the line which states **Going, Maybe, Invited**. Otherwise, for a public event, click the line **Going, Interested, Invited**

3 A window will appear, split into sections. Look under

the categories (for example with a private event, Going, Maybe, Invited and Can't Go) and see who is listed in each. You can also use the Search bar to find specific guests to quickly check their response

4 If anyone is listed who you would rather not be part of your event, click **Remove** to the right of their name

Altering the description of the event and adding co-hosts

Should you need to amend your event, Facebook allows you to edit the details you created when you set it up. This is great if, for example, your birthday party has suddenly become a joint celebration, or if you need to clarify a misleading description.

1 In the box which states the name of your event, click the button marked **Edit**

2 Make your amends. You can alter the time and location if you wish

3 You can also add a **co-host** if you need help in running the event. Include their name in the Co-hosts section

4 Click **Save**

If you decide to add a co-host, then they will be able to edit your event details and invite others.

Facebook doesn't allow you to formally change an event from private to public, but if you select Duplicate via the three-dot menu on your event listing you can change the privacy setting and resubmit it.

Share the event on your own Timeline, or in your Group or Page. If you want to spread the word further, ask others to share it as well.

Building some excitement

Don't just set up an event and leave it to chance that people will engage with it. Keep adding content to create a buzz, and encourage others to share it. This is particularly important if your event is a public one.

1 On your event page, you will see a box that allows you to write posts, add photos and videos, and create polls. It is effectively a cut-down version of the Create a Post box that you use to engage with people on your own Timeline

2 To write a post, simply type into the section labeled **Write something...**

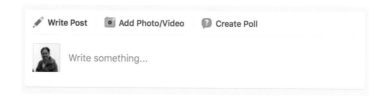

3 To engage using visuals, click **Add Photo/Video**. Click the large **+** box, or select the Camera icon to look for an image or video on your computer. You are able to say something about the image, while tagging people, using emojis and adding a location marker

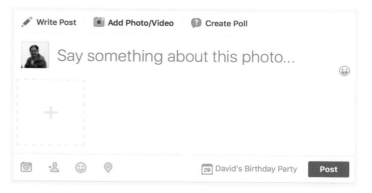

4 Click **Create Poll** and you can ask a question. Click **Add Poll Options** to suggest some possible answers

5 Click **Post** when you are finished

Creating a QR code

Another good way of promoting an event is to create a QR code. These work like the barcodes you'll find on everyday items in the shop and they can be scanned using the camera on your smartphone, as long as you are using a QR reader app. The codes can be generated for public events, allowing you to use them on posters and other promotional material.

1 Go to the page for your event

2 Click the three-dot menu in the top-right corner

3 Choose Create QR code from the drop-down menu

4 You will now see the QR code on the screen. Click Download to save it to your computer

5 You can now use an art package to place the code within any promotional material you wish to create such as a poster, leaflet or glossy brochure

Cancel and delete events

If you decide you don't want to go ahead with an event, you can cancel it. Facebook will let you inform all of the guests and you can choose if you wish to delete everything posted to the event.

1 Click **Edit** on the page for your event

2 Select **Cancel Event** at the very bottom of the Edit window

3 If you choose to cancel the event by selecting the button next to **Cancel**, you will be able to add a post to the Event page, explaining your decision and what people should do

4 If you select the button next to **Delete** instead, all of the posts will be erased. In both cases, guests will be notified

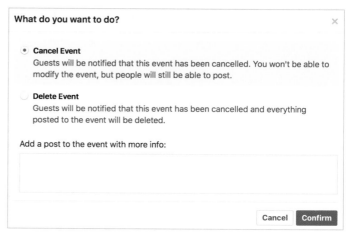

5 Click **Confirm**

6 Note that canceled or deleted events won't be listed under the Past section on the main Event page

10 Using photos and videos

Earlier chapters have touched on how you can upload images and videos to Facebook, but these pages show ways of editing your media and creating albums.

Upload photos and videos

They've long said a picture paints a thousand words, and that is very much true here. Indeed, photos and videos are a key part of Facebook's appeal. They let you share a snapshot of your life, and they allow you to put funny images and cartoons out there for all to see.

You can find out more about the basics of uploading photos and videos on pages 48 and 49.

1 Click or tap **Photo** or **Photo/Video** in the Create a Post box at the top of your News Feed or Timeline, depending on whether you are accessing Facebook on your computer or mobile device

2 You can now browse for an image or video on your computer or device, clicking or tapping any media that you want to share with others

3 Write something about the image or video

4 If you need to add more images, you can click the **+** button

5 Select the drop-down marked Friends, and choose who can see your post

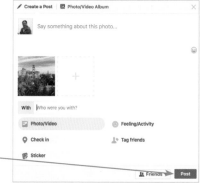

6 Click or tap **Post** when you are ready

Adding tags to photos

If your image contains people, Facebook can pick up on their faces and allow you to tag them. Essentially, this means you are able to put a name to the face, and it's a nice way of identifying who has been photographed while letting the people you have tagged know an image of them has been posted.

1 Upload a photo to Facebook

2 If you are accessing Facebook via a browser, hover over the image you uploaded, and click the Tag button ————

3 This will let you see the image on a full screen. You will notice that boxes will have been placed around the heads of any people in the photo. Also note that if you are using Facebook on a mobile device, this will happen automatically (as in the image to the right)

4 Click or tap the box, and type in the name of the person pictured. On the browser version of Facebook, thumbnails of anyone in the photo will be placed down the left-hand side. Click **Who is this?** to fill in their details

5 Click **Save** or **Done**

6 When anyone views the image, they will be able to see exactly who is pictured. The people included will also be informed they've been tagged

When you tag someone in a photo, the image may appear on their News Feed, depending on their security settings.

Facebook uses clever face-recognition technology to suggest tags.

Editing your photographs

Facebook has its own image-editing suite. It is nowhere near as sophisticated as dedicated software such as Photoshop, but it will allow you to crop your images and add filters, stickers and text.

1 Upload your photo to your computer, hover over it in the Create a Post box and click **Edit Photo**

2 Facebook's editing suite will then appear on the screen

Using the Filters

Filters allow you to make instant alterations to the overall look of your images.

1 Click **Filters** from the left-hand menu

2 Click any of the filters, ranging from Vintage, Spring and Summer to Autumn, Winter and Snow

3 Your image will change straightaway but if you don't like what you see, you can revert back by clicking Original

Cropping your images

Perhaps the most useful editing tool is Crop. It lets you home in on a particular section of your image and remove sections which get in the way. You can also rotate your image here.

1 Click **Crop** from the left-hand menu

2 A grid will be placed over your image to help you align the photo. Click and hold the circles located in the four corners of the grid over the part of the image you want to retain

3 You can toggle the grid from its rectangular original to a square to alter the shape of the photo

4 You can also click **Rotate** to quickly rotate the image one 90-degree angle at a time

Adding text

1 Click **Text** from the left-hand menu

2 Click **Add Text** and start typing

3 Click a color to the left to alter the color of your text

The spellings in Facebook are determined by your Language settings.

4 Click **Left** or **Centered** to left-justify or center the text

5 Click the drop-down box to change the font

...cont'd

Adding Stickers

Stickers can help to lift an image. They will be overlaid onto your image.

1 Click **Stickers** from the left-hand menu

2 In the window that appears, search for the sticker that you want to use

3 When the sticker appears on the screen, move it into position, altering its size using the blue arrow

4 Click elsewhere on the image to lock it into place. If you want to move it again, simply re-click it. Click X to delete the sticker

Resizing your images

1 Click the slider at the bottom of the editing window

2 Move it left to make the image smaller and move it right to enlarge it

Finishing off

Once you have completed editing your image:

● Click **Save** in the bottom right-hand corner of the screen.

● Or, if you want to abandon the lot, click **Cancel**.

Share 360-degree photos

In recent years, 360-degree photographs have become very popular since they are more immersive than standard images. Facebook allows you to snap and share these photos on a mobile device. Viewers can then look around the virtual environments, either by dragging a finger around the screen or by moving the device.

1 Open the Camera app or a dedicated 360-degree app on your device, and take a panoramic photograph

2 Open the Facebook app and in the Create a Post box, select **Photo/Video**. Choose the image you wish to share

3 When you tap **Post**, the 360-degree shot will be available to view

4 Others can then view the image by moving their finger around the screen. A Compass icon will appear on the image to show that it was taken in 360 degrees. The device's gyroscope will also allow you to move the device around to see more of the photo. You can use your mouse if you are viewing the content on your computer

Uploading 360-degree video

If you have a camera capable of taking 360-degree video such as an Insta360 Nano, Gear 360 or LG 360 CAM (R105), you can upload the footage in the same way as above.

Hot tip

You see lots of samples of 360-degree content on the Facebook 360 Community Page at https://www.facebook.com/groups/facebook360community

Hot tip

Do you have a Samsung Gear VR headset and a compatible phone? Then tap the downward arrow on a 360-degree image and select View in VR to see it in virtual reality.

Editing images on mobiles

The same editing features discussed on pages 140-143 are also available on the app.

1 Upload an image and click **Edit**, which you will see displayed on the photo

2 Tap the options at the bottom of the screen:

- Select **Filter** and swipe the photo to see each one in Android, or select from the filters at the bottom of the screen in iOS.

- Select **Crop** before tapping and dragging the circles on the corner of your image to select the part of the image you want.

- Select **Text** and use the keyboard to write your words, selecting a color from the right of the screen.

- Select **Stickers**, choose an image and place it.

Doodling on your images
The mobile app adds an extra feature: the ability to draw freehand over your images.

1 After uploading the image and tapping Edit, select **Doodle** from the bottom of the screen

2 Tap the color you want from the right-hand side

3 Begin to draw with your finger on the image

4 Tap **Save** when you are finished in Android, and **Done** in iOS

Creating an album

As well as uploading a single photo or even a series of videos, you can also create and group them within an album.

1 In the Create a Post box, click **Photo/Video Album**

2 Choose the images or videos that you wish to include in the album you're about to create

3 The Create album window will appear

4 Fill in the boxes to the left with the album name, a description and, optionally, the location where the images and videos were taken

5 Click **+ Add Photos/Videos** to place more media into the album. When you have finished, select who should see the album, and click **Post**

Why not let friends add their own images to your album? Click **Add contributors** in the Create album window and enter their names.

If you want the album to be for your eyes only, select **Only me** when choosing who should be able to view it.

Click Photos from the left-hand menu of your News Feed to view any albums that you create.

Managing your albums

To view your albums, click Photos in the left-hand menu of your News Feed. You will see tabs for Your Photos and Albums.

Adding to an album

You can also add written posts to an album.

1 Click the Create a Post box, and select **+Album**

2 Select the album you wish to add to, and click **Photo/Video Album** to add images or videos to it

3 Click **Post**

Downloading, moving and making use of images

Once you have uploaded an image to an album, you are able to perform a number of tasks such as being able to download it, get a link to it, move it to another album or delete it.

Using Get Link is particularly useful for sharing an image with someone who doesn't use Facebook. Simply paste the link in an email or message, and send it.

1 Select the album you want to manage

2 Hover over the photograph with your mouse, and select the **Edit** button

Like · Comment   5   2

3 You will see this menu. It allows you to add a location and change the date of the image. Clicking Download will instantly save a copy to your computer

📍 Add Location
⏱ Change Date
Download
Make Profile Picture
Make Cover Photo
Make Featured Photo
Make Album Cover
Get Link
Move To Other Album
Delete This Photo

4 There are options to make the image your profile picture, cover photo, featured photo or album cover

5 Click the final section's options to get a link, move it to another album or delete

Broadcasting live videos

Facebook Live has proven to be very popular, allowing you to broadcast videos in real time. You can create a live broadcast from your computer or phone.

1 Click **Live Video** in the Create a Post box on your computer. Or, tap **Live** on iOS or **Go Live** on Android

2 Allow access to your camera and microphone, and choose the camera you want to use (in the case of a mobile, you'd select either the front or the back)

3 Describe your live video

4 Select who should be able to see your broadcast by tapping the **Friends** drop-down menu

5 Click **Go Live** to begin broadcasting for as long as four hours

Watching a live broadcast

1 When you begin a live broadcast, your friends will be notified that they can tune in to watch you. The same goes for when they create a live broadcast: you can watch them too. The action takes place in the News Feed, and others are able to react by making comments and sending emoji reactions

2 You can also discover live videos from across the world by visiting **https://www.facebook.com/livemap** and clicking on any of the blue dots you see

Hot tip

You can choose between a video broadcast or audio-only. Tap the Camera icon on the Live screen to toggle between the two.

Hot tip

If you are watching a Facebook Live video and you are deaf or hard of hearing, you may be able to view closed captions. With Facebook on your computer, click the downward arrow in the top-right corner, select Videos in the left-hand menu and turn **Always Show Captions** to On.

Keep an eye on this app: Facebook has been offering live coverage of events and sports.

You can sit back and allow videos to automatically play one after another.

Viewing videos on your TV

Facebook has created a special app, Facebook Video, which lets you watch videos from your News Feed along with others that it thinks you may like. The app is available for Apple TV and Android TV.

Installing the app

1 If you have an Apple TV device hooked up to your television, navigate to its App Store and look for Facebook Video. Click the **Install** button

2 If you have an Android TV device such as SHIELD TV or Nexus Player, go to Google Play and search for Facebook Video, and select to **Install**

3 Open the app, and click **Log in with Facebook**

4 You will see a code on the screen. Either go to **facebook. com/device** in a computer browser and input the code, or tap the notification sent to your Facebook mobile app

5 Confirm the device can receive your public profile

Using the app

1 Various sections run down the left-hand column, including Suggested,

Live, Games and Your videos. Select any of these to view a host of videos in the right-hand part of the screen

2 Use your device's remote to select a video. Sit back and watch

3 Click Search in the left-hand menu to find specific videos

11 Buying and selling

Although the likes of eBay and Gumtree are very popular online marketplaces, this chapter explores using Facebook as a way of selling your items and potentially picking up a bargain.

Introducing the Marketplace

As well as allowing you to keep up to speed with what your friends are doing, and to message and join groups, Facebook also lets you buy and sell items. You can:

Hot tip

Facebook does not take a cut of any money spent on Marketplace.

- Discover the items that people close by have listed for sale.

- Narrow down your searches by category, location or price.

- Learn more about the various sellers and communicate with them by direct message.

It is a great way to have a clear-out and make some money and, since items tend to be cheaper than in the shops, it is a lovely way of saving some cash too. Many people use it to look for items that are unavailable in the shops. It is rapidly growing in popularity.

Opening the Marketplace on a mobile device
To open the Marketplace on a smartphone or tablet:

1 Ensure that you have the latest version of the Facebook app installed so that you will have the most up-to-date Marketplace that's available

2 Tap this icon, which you will see either at the top or bottom of the screen, depending on the mobile version that you are using

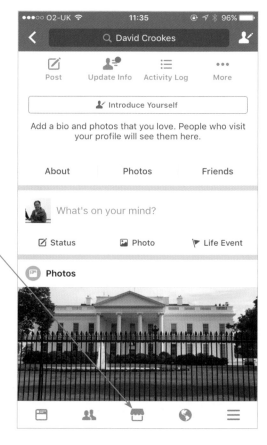

Opening the Marketplace on a computer

When the service launched it was originally only available to use on a mobile, but you can now use it on a desktop computer too.

The larger screen of a PC or Mac makes it easier for you to see the items you are thinking about buying.

1 Go to **facebook.com** in a browser on your computer and log in

2 Click the **Marketplace** icon in the left-hand menu

3 You will be taken straight to the Marketplace Home screen, from where you will be able to browse the items that are on offer and sell something of your own

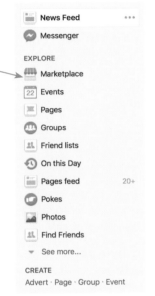

Paying for items bought, and receiving cash for items sold

If you have ever bought or sold an item online, then it's likely you will have done so using eBay. This service relies, to a great extent, on the online payment service PayPal, which lets users send and receive cash quickly and easily without needing to divulge any actual payment card details.

With Facebook Marketplace, you and a seller (or you and a buyer) are left to sort out the payment details yourself. You could use PayPal but there is no automatic link from the Marketplace for such a service, so you have to go direct to **paypal.com** or use the PayPal app. Alternatively, you could try other online payment services, or arrange a personal visit and complete the transaction with cash.

Beware

Don't send money to someone online unless you are 100 per cent confident the person is trustworthy. Facebook advises face-to-face Marketplace transactions.

Discover items for sale

If you are looking for an item to buy on Facebook Marketplace, there are various features to help you to find what you are after. These allow you to search for something specific, or else browse according to the category which best takes your fancy.

Finding Marketplace items on a mobile

Hot tip

When a seller reduces the price of an item, this will be flagged up clearly in the listings, helping you to identify some potential bargains.

Search marketplace. By tapping the Search bar, you are able to type in a search query.

Categories button. Tap this to call up a list of categories and sub-categories, ranging from Home and Entertainment to Hobbies and Family.

Individual category buttons. You can also swipe along this section and tap an individual category. Doing so takes you direct to the relevant page of listings.

Location button. By default, Marketplace will show items based on your current location. You can change this by tapping it.

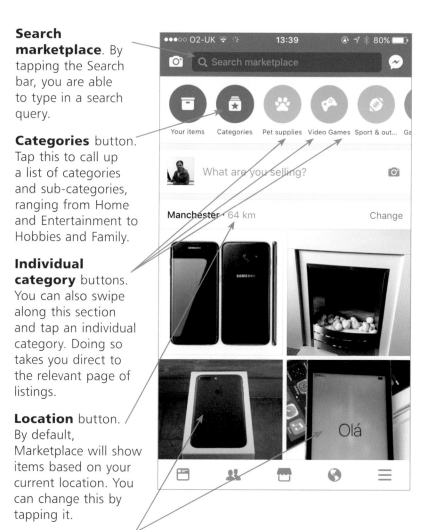

Listings. Each of these images represents a product you can buy from another Marketplace user. To see more listings, simply scroll down the screen, and they will appear.

Note that while the screen above has been taken from the iOS version, the features are the same for Android.

Finding Marketplace items on a computer

Browse button. Clicking this will let you see the items that are currently on sale.

Search Marketplace. If you need to search for a specific item, use this bar.

Filters. Click the Location, Price and Category buttons to narrow or expand your searches.

Hot tip

You can set your location from as close as 2km away to as far as 100km via the location filter.

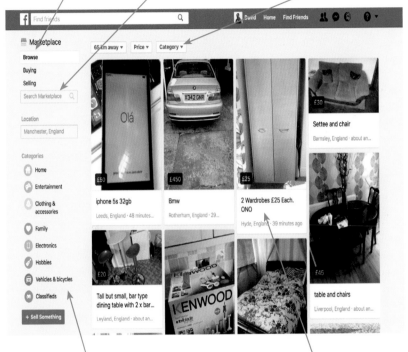

Category buttons. Click on the categories, and they will expand to show you a number of sub-categories. Each helps to narrow your search further.

Listings. These entries show an image of the product, the price, a brief description, the time of posting, and the item's location.

Setting a specific price bracket for searches

1 Click the filter marked **Price** at the top of the screen

2 Select a minimum and maximum price

3 Click **Apply**

Hot tip

If you see two or more dots at the bottom of an image, it means there is more than one photo available. Scroll or click to see them all.

Hot tip

Keep an eye out for sellers who are marked as being Very Responsive. Since they typically reply to messages within an hour, you may enjoy a less troublesome transaction.

Examining the product pages

Each item listed on Facebook's Marketplace contains the same vital information that will help you to make an informed purchasing decision:

- A description of the item, including a photograph.

- The location from which it is being sold, including a map.

- The date it was uploaded to the Marketplace.

- The price at which it is being sold.

- The number of people who have viewed the item.

- Its state: i.e. whether or not it is new and boxed.

- The profile image and name of the seller.

- An option to message the seller.

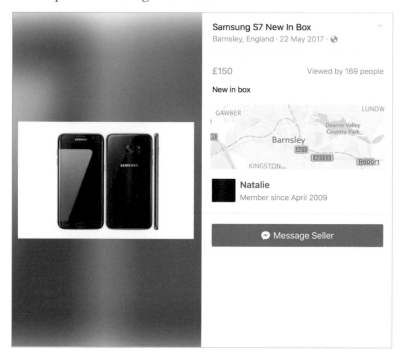

Enjoy extra features on mobile

The mobile app version also lets you **Save** and **Share** a listing.

By tapping the profile of a seller, you can view someone's Marketplace activity and see what else they are currently selling.

Sending sellers a message

If you like the look of an item but you need more information, you can send the seller a direct message.

Using the app

1 Click or tap the item you want to buy on the listing page

2 Select **Message Seller**

3 You could choose from one of four pre-determined messages suggested by Facebook:

- I'm interested in this item.
- Is this item still available?
- What condition is this item in?
- Do you deliver?

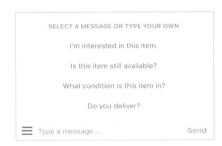

4 Alternatively, write your own message. Tap the option **Type a message**

5 Tap **Send**

Using a computer

1 Click the item you want, and select **Message Seller**

2 The desktop version displays some default words. You can edit them if you wish by clicking the box

3 Tap **Send Message**

Beware

Avoid sharing any financial information in your message, and don't give out your email address or phone number to a seller.

Hot tip

After you have messaged the seller, keep an eye on your notifications for a reply.

Beware

Purchases made on Marketplace are not protected by Facebook.

Making an offer on an item

As well as sending a direct message to a seller, you can also make an offer when using the app. If you do:

● Avoid upsetting a seller by ensuring your offer is reasonable: do some homework by looking around to see how much the item tends to sell for on sites such as eBay and Craigslist, and elsewhere on Marketplace.

● Ensure it is an offer that, should it be accepted, you'd be willing to go ahead with.

● Be absolutely certain that what you will get is what you are expecting. In other words, check the listing and communicate with the seller if there is any doubt.

1 Click on **Make Offer**

2 If using iOS, the amount asked for by the seller will be displayed. Use the numerical on-screen keyboard to delete the amount and then tap in the sum that you want the seller to consider

Asking price: £150

£ **150**

Send Offer

1	2 ABC	3 DEF
4 GHI	5 JKL	6 MNO
7 PQRS	8 TUV	9 WXYZ
	0	⌫

3 If you are using Android, a pre-written message will appear instead. You can alter the offer price by deleting the amount and inserting your own

4 Tap **Send Offer** in iOS or **Send** in Android. Now wait for the offer to be accepted or declined, but be patient while the seller considers the amount you have put forward

Creating your own item post

Do you have some items that you would like to sell? You can quickly create your own post on Marketplace.

Using the app

1 Click **What are your selling?** or **Sell Something**, depending on the platform you're using

2 If you have already taken a photo of your item using your mobile device, choose one or more images from your Camera Roll, and tap Next

3 Alternatively, take a new photo of your item. Tap the **Camera** button and press the Shutter button when ready

4 Type the title of your item using up to 100 characters. Tap Next

5 Describe the item. The more detailed you are, the more chance of selling. Tap **Next**

6 Set a price, and tap **Next**

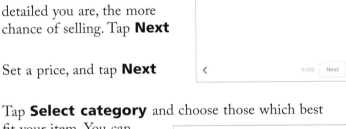

7 Tap **Select category** and choose those which best fit your item. You can change your current location by tapping its name and dragging the map to show your locality

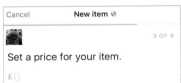

8 Decide if you also want to post to your profile or other groups by tapping **Your Profile** or on any other groups that appear

9 Tap **Post**

It's a good idea to check out how the buying process works before posting your own item.

Selling via the website? Simply tap **Sell Something** at the bottom of the left-hand menu, and the selling options described here will appear on a single pop-up form. Fill in the sections, and click **Post**.

Keep track of items you sell

Once you have listed your items, you will need to keep track of them. Marketplace makes it easy to see which of your items are available and which have sold, and it brings all of the messages relating to your items in one place.

1 Tap the button for **Your items**

2 Tap the **Selling** tab to see all of your listings

3 Those listed under Active are still available to buy. You'll see a thumbnail image of the item, its title and the price

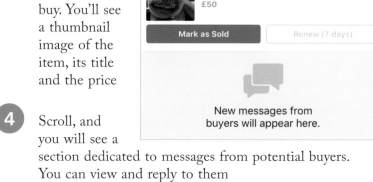

4 Scroll, and you will see a section dedicated to messages from potential buyers. You can view and reply to them

Mark an item as sold

When you sell an item, you have to manually mark it as having been sold. It's a good idea to do this because it removes the item from sale, and it also makes it easy to see which items you still need to sell.

1 Underneath each item listing, you will see an option for **Mark as Sold**. Tap it

2 You can, if you wish, reverse this by selecting **Mark as Available** at a later date

Editing your item listings

Have you made a mistake with your listing? Do you need to remove it? Or, would you like to post it to somewhere else as well? You can do all of these things.

You can use as many as 10 photos in your listings, so don't hold back.

1 Within the Selling tab of Your items, find the item you want to edit and tap the three-dot menu next to it

2 You will see three options. If you would like to remove a listing, tap **Delete Item**

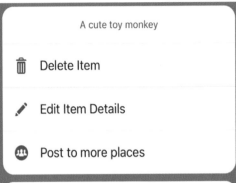

A cute toy monkey

🗑 Delete Item

✏ Edit Item Details

♨ Post to more places

Cancel

3 To edit a listing, tap **Edit Item Details**. Make the necessary changes, and tap Post when you're done

4 If you want to post the listing to your profile or other groups, tap **Post to more places** and choose where you would your listing to be

Keeping track of items and editing on the website

You are also able to monitor the items you are selling on the Marketplace website.

The tab for Selling is found in the left-hand Menu bar.

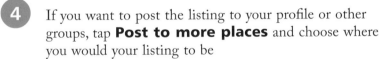

🛒 Marketplace   Active   **Sold**

Browse

Buying

Selling

This will activate a page that splits your items into Active and Sold. Click the two tabs at the top of the page to switch between the two sections.

The website lets you delete, edit and repost listings too. This is good news for anyone who prefers to work on a larger screen.

Beware

Bear in mind that some people would avoid listings that are littered with poor grammar and spelling mistakes.

Get a good price for items

Whether you are buying or selling, you'll want to pay or receive a good price for items. Here are some tips:

- **Be prepared for negotiation.** If you are buying an item, don't be afraid to put in an offer that is less than the asking price. The seller can only say no. Similarly, be open to people asking for your items for less. One way to combat this is to price your items a little bit higher. Not so high that it puts people off from buying, though.

- **Get the images right.** Photos sell an item, so make sure that any you take are sharp and showcase the item well. That means ditching blurred images and taking a few of them against clean backgrounds in good light. Poor images will usually result in lower offers, so why not take advantage of that if you see a listing accompanied by a bad photo?

- **Check the description.** Selling an item? Then go into detail so that a buyer can be confident that they know what they will be getting. A good description that covers every question you can think of can also prevent you from being bombarded by quizzical buyers. Buying an item? Then look carefully at what you're getting, and ensure you'll receive value for money.

- **Pay with cash.** Never send cash in the post or wire money to a stranger. But do consider meeting with a buyer or seller and using cash rather than an online payment service. Companies such as PayPal are secure and convenient, but there may be fees involved. Cash transactions can save money for both buyers and sellers. Perhaps offer a discount if someone is willing to pay with notes and coins, and ask for one if you're buying in this way.

- **Stay safe.** You can't put a price on personal safety, so if you do meet up with someone you have met on the Marketplace, do so in a crowded public place.

12 Tailoring the adverts

Facebook is funded by advertising, but you can change the settings to determine what you do and don't get to see.

Beware

You can adjust the advert settings but you cannot avoid seeing ads.

Accessing the advert settings

Facebook is free to use but, since it has to be paid for in some way, it may not be surprising to learn that advertising brings in the bulk of the social network's revenue.

This is no bad thing. Facebook is, after all, a very useful service and its adverts are mostly unobtrusive. But you should still keep a check on the adverts that are being served to you.

How are advertisers targeting you?

Facebook is attractive to advertisers because they are able to tap into data about the network's users. It allows businesses to target you with adverts that are relevant not only to the things you like, but also the area in which you live, your age, your gender, and more. This increases the chance of you engaging with an advertiser.

As you can guess, much of this relies on the information that you are "giving away" on the social network. When you click Like on a post, for instance, Check in at a location or use the mobile app, Facebook can get a more rounded view of you.

And yet it's important to note that Facebook is not being sinister. It is transparent about what it collects and does with your data, and it is clear about what it won't do (it won't read your emails, for instance).

Still, Facebook's reach can be wide. Businesses can install code on their websites that records when you visit, or cross-reference the email or phone number you use on Facebook with any records they have themselves.

Visiting the advertising settings on Facebook

1　Click the downward arrow in the top-right corner

2　Select **Settings**

    Apps
    Ads
    Payments
    Support Inbox
    Videos

3　Click **Ads** in the left-hand menu

4　You will now be on the advert preferences page

Configure your interests

The first section you will see is Your interests. It is made up of items gathered as you make use of Facebook. For example, liking a page related to the Victorian era created an entry in this section for that very subject. Liking a page related to cats produced an entry for felines. Looking at what Facebook thinks you are interested in should be your first port of call.

Adverts are not generally targeted at you on the basis of a single preference. Other criteria are also used.

1 Click **Your interests**

2 Go through the various categories, which can range from business and industry to food and drink. Click More to see extra categories

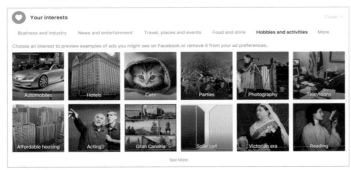

3 Hover over a subject, and it will tell you why

About Photography
You have this preference because you clicked on an ad related to Photography.

the preference is listed. In our case, we apparently clicked an advert related to Photography

4 Click the subject, for example adverts targeting people with this preference

5 Think you would benefit from the adverts? Click the smiling face at the bottom of the window. If not, click the unsmiling face

Hot tip

By reporting advertisers which have delivered a bad experience, you could (if your reasons are valid, of course) help others in the future.

See who you've engaged with

Whenever you engage with an advertiser, Facebook makes a note or it, allowing other advertisers with a similar remit to potentially send ads your way. Again, to ensure that the information Facebook has about you is accurate, you should check the data that has been gathered.

1 Click **Advertisers you've interacted with**

2 There are three categories of advertiser to click on:

- Those you have interacted with using your contact information. This means the email or phone number you are using on Facebook is included on the customer list of a business.

- Those whose websites or app you have used. This relates to advertisers you have actively engaged with that make use of Facebook technology.

- Those whose ads you have clicked.

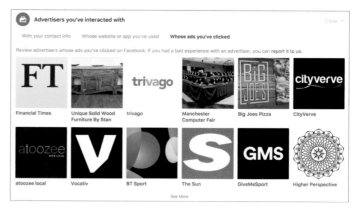

3 Hover over each entry and you will see a box appear in its corner. An X is displayed for entries in the first two categories. You are able to click and **Remove** the entry

4 A downward arrow shows for entries in the third category. Click and select **Report** to report the advertiser, or **Hide** to hide any adverts from them

Checking your personal info

Advertisers can make use of information contained on your profile, but you can determine what can and cannot be used.

1 Click **Your information**

2 Click **About you**

3 You will see that Facebook advertisers can make use of your relationship status, employer, job title and education. Next to entries for these is a slider which you can turn on or off (blue for on). Decide what you want advertisers to have access to

As Facebook itself explains, any amendments made to your information under About you does not mean the details are hidden from view.

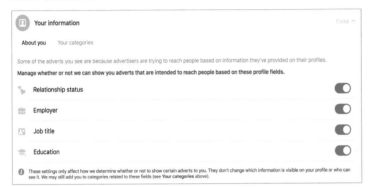

4 Click **Your categories**

5 Information obtained by Facebook through your use of the site is shown. It can include your birthday, the browser you tend to use, your generation, or the devices you access Facebook on. Hover over each entry for more details

6 Remove any details by hovering the mouse over the item, then clicking **X** next to each entry

Alter your advert settings

Here, we are looking at a section which asks you three questions with the aim of making the adverts work better for you.

1 Click **Advert settings**

2 The first question asks whether you would like to see adverts based on your use of websites and apps. This is relevant because Facebook allows websites and apps to use its tracking software, and those that do are able to gather data which the social network can then use to work out which ads are most relevant for you. There are benefits: if you were looking for a new phone, you may see adverts on Facebook promoting good deals. But if you want to turn this off, click **Yes**, select **Choose Settings** and click **No**. Reverse this process to activate it again

3 The next question asks if you want to see ads on apps and websites from the Facebook Companies. This allows the information gathered about you on Facebook, and from companies which use its tracking software, to display adverts on websites and apps that are not linked to the social network. If you want to turn this off, select **Yes**, click the drop-down box displaying **Yes**, and click **No**. Again, reverse this process to reactivate it

4 Finally, you will be asked if you want others to see "adverts with your social

actions". This means your friends will see adverts from companies you have liked, shared and commented on (such as in the image here). Adverts will also depend on the events you join and your app usage. If you don't want anyone to see adverts based on how you interact with a particular business, select **My friends only,** click the drop-down box, and select **No one**. Reverse this to reactivate

Using another ad opt-out

As well as altering the settings on Facebook itself, you are also able to opt out of seeing interest-based advertising from Facebook in your current browser.

1 Go to **http://optout.aboutads.info** to access the website of the Digital Advertising Alliance (DAA) and make sure cookies are enabled

2 It will perform a check of your browser before showing you a list of companies participating in the DAA's WebChoices tool. The companies marked Yes will have customized ads enabled on your browser

3 Look down the list for Facebook. Click **+** to see more information and, to stop it from customizing ads on your browser, tick the box to the right. You can, if you wish, click **Opt Out Of All** at the bottom of the screen

4 Click **Submit your choices**

Hiding advertisements from view

If you see a particular advert and you'd rather not view it again, you can select to hide it and tell Facebook you don't like it.

1 Click the downward arrow in the top-right of an advert

2 Select **Hide ad**

3 You can also select **This ad is useful** if you actually like it and want to see more

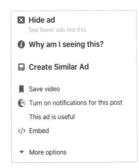

Hot tip

You can also use ad blockers on mobiles, tablets and computers. Popular choices include Adblock Plus, Ghostery and HTTPS Everywhere.

If an advert directs you to a different website than the one advertised, immediately close the browser tab.

Watching out for fakes

Facebook does all it can to keep you safe, and it will never knowingly serve you fake advertisements. Sometimes, though, a rogue ad may slip through the net and there have been cases of domain names being spoofed to mislead you into clicking; the aim being to direct you to a different website.

You may also see spoof offers that are unwittingly shared by others. Facebook will block all such offenders, but be wary too.

Spotting fakes

The image on this page was not placed as an advert but it fooled some people into sharing it. Those behind it hoped people would click. Websites, however, can contain viruses or look to trick you into revealing your details. Not everything is quite what it seems.

Encouraging offer. This UK supermarket was said to be giving £75 vouchers to everyone to celebrate its anniversary. That's a lot of money, and alarm bells should have started ringing straightaway.

Wrong date. Sure, it expired on May 15, 2017 but people in the UK don't use the month-day-year format, preferring day-month-year.

Low-res image. The image is blurry which isn't very professional.

Asda is giving free £75 Vouchers to EVERYONE For their Anniversary!!
www.asda-n29g18o.gbyes.us

Bad grammar. A genuine offer (or news story about an offer) would at least get the grammar right. The use of capitals, the capped-up "For", "their" instead of "its", and the two exclamation marks all look suspect.

Odd website address. Asda's website is **asda.com**. This website fails to match that, and it looks strange with its jumble of numbers and letters and a .us suffix. Even if it is a "news story" about the coupon, it looks odd.

13 Privacy and security

If you are concerned that your personal life is being overly exposed on Facebook, then this chapter looks at the various ways you are able to maintain your privacy.

You should also consider the privacy of others in the posts you create.

Parents, educators and guardians can visit **https://www.facebook. com/safety** to learn more about keeping children safe online.

170

Keeping your privacy intact

Facebook is a social network that encourages you to share your thoughts, day-to-day activities, likes and interests. As such, many people have expressed concerns about privacy and there has been, in recent times, a noticeable fall in the number of users making posts about their own life.

To address this and to continue making the network a personal experience, Facebook has worked on ways of making it easier for you to control your level of privacy. Before we look at those, however, you should consider some common-sense steps for an easier and more private online life.

- Always remember that anything you post on Facebook is typically shared with a wide group of people, some of whom may not be your closest friends. If you wouldn't share something publicly in the real world, think carefully about sharing it on social media.

- It is possible for anyone to take a screenshot. So even if you post something you later regret, deleting it may not solve the issue. Anyone who has taken a screenshot could share it. Again, this comes back to thinking carefully about what you are posting before you press that button.

- Be wary of giving away too much about your whereabouts. You may want to share those pictures of yourself on holiday while you are away or tell all that you're at a concert, but security experts would suggest you wait until you get back. Burglars have been known to keep an eye on Facebook.

- Similarly, don't brag about new purchases or your possessions, and keep a close eye on the personal details you have listed on the site. Are you giving too much away: the name of your school or date of birth, perhaps? Such information can be used for identity fraud or to get past online security questions.

- Consider your reputation. Think about what you are sharing, posting and liking, and how others may view you for doing so. Employers often look at social media to get an indication of your character. Your views may not necessarily tally with those they hold, regardless of where on the political spectrum you may be, or the opinions you hold.

Take a privacy checkup

The quickest way to keep an eye on your privacy settings is to use Facebook's Privacy Checkup feature. It takes you through a small number of steps so that you can review who should be able to view the items you post.

1 Click the Question Mark icon in the top-right corner of Facebook, and select **Privacy Checkup**

2 Alter who is able to view your next post by clicking the drop-down menu (which will be highlighted the first time you use it) and choosing from Friends, Public, Friends except, Only me and Specific friends

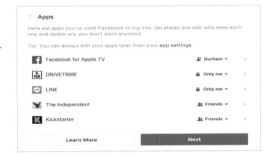

3 Click **Next**

4 The more you use Facebook, the more likely you will use it to log into various apps. Choose who can see the apps you've

used by clicking the downward arrow and choosing from Only me, Public, Friends and Custom. Select More Options to see some extra choices. Click **X** to delete apps

5 Click **Next**

6 Look at the information stored on your profile. Choose who you want to see it by clicking the downward arrow

7 Click **Finish Up**

Hot tip

You can also quickly check who sees your posts by clicking the Question Mark icon and selecting Privacy.

Check who sees your posts

There are some basic privacy settings that you need to take a look at to make sure they work well for you, starting with looking at who can see your stuff.

1 Click the Question Mark icon in the top-right corner, and select **Settings**

2 Click **Privacy** from the left-hand menu

3 You have four options available to you:

- **Who can see your future posts?** Click Edit, and choose the group of people you'd like to open or limit your posts to.

- **Who can see your friends list?** Click Edit, and choose who should see your list. Selecting Only me ensures others can only view your mutual friends.

- **Review all your posts and things you're tagged in** Click Use Activity Log, and you will be shown a list of stories you have been mentioned in. You can select to Hide items or Add to Timeline.

- **Limit the audience for posts you've shared with friends of friends or Public?** By selecting this and clicking Limit Past Posts, every past post will only be viewable by Friends unless you have tagged people, in which case they and their friends will be able to view too.

4 Click **Close** when you have finished with each section. You are now able to move on to who can contact you and look you up

Configure who can see you

Facebook also allows you to determine who is able to contact you and who is able to look you up.

1 Click the Question Mark icon in the top-right corner, and select **Settings**

2 Click **Privacy** from the left-hand menu

3 Configure **Who can send you friend requests?** by clicking **Edit** next to this option. You can limit it to Friends of friends if you wish

4 You can also determine who can look you up:

- **Who can look you up using the email address you provided?** It is possible for people to search for you by inputting your email address in the Search bar. You can only choose Friends, Friends of friends, or Everyone. You can't select no-one.

- **Who can look you up using the phone number you provided?** Again, people can search for you by inputting your phone number into the Search bar. Choose Friends, Friends of friends, or Everyone. You can't select no-one here, either.

- **Do you want search engines outside of Facebook to link to your profile?** This is unticked by default, so only click it if you don't mind search engines such as Google being able to link to your profile in their results.

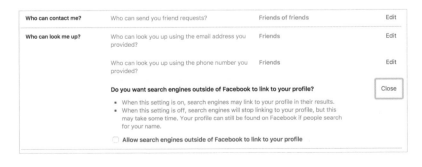

Who can contact me?	Who can send you friend requests?	Friends of friends	Edit
Who can look me up?	Who can look you up using the email address you provided?	Friends	Edit
	Who can look you up using the phone number you provided?	Friends	Edit
	Do you want search engines outside of Facebook to link to your profile?		Close
	• When this setting is on, search engines may link to your profile in their results. • When this setting is off, search engines will stop linking to your profile, but this may take some time. Your profile can still be found on Facebook if people search for your name.		
	☐ Allow search engines outside of Facebook to link to your profile		

Control and review posts

It is also important to check what others can add to your Timeline and who is able to view what is posted on there. By changing the settings, you can exert greater control and give yourself the ultimate say over what appears. This can prevent others from posting embarrassing things as well as items that breach your privacy.

1 Click the Question Mark icon in the top-right corner, and select **Settings**

2 Click **Timeline and Tagging** from the left-hand menu

Determine who can add stuff to your Timeline

The first section lets you decide who can post to your Timeline, and whether or not you want to review those posts before they appear for others to see.

1 Click **Edit** next to **Who can post on your Timeline?** then click the audience selector. By choosing Only me you are able to prevent others from posting to your Timeline

Who can add things to my Timeline?	Who can post on your Timeline?	Friends	Edit
	Review posts friends tag you in before they appear on your Timeline?	On	Edit

2 Click Edit next to **Review posts friends tag you in before they appear on your Timeline?** Choose Enabled or Disabled from the drop-down menu. Enabling means you are notified when someone tags you in a post

3 You will be able to decide if you want to hide other people's posts from your Timeline or add them. To do this, click the downward arrow at the top of Facebook, and select **Activity Log**

4 Click **Timeline Review** from the left-hand menu, then go down the list, clicking Hide or Add to Timeline

Select what others can see

In this section, you are able to review what others see on your Timeline, and control who sees posts you've been tagged in and who can see what others post. These latter two options are particularly useful if you are allowing anyone to post to your Timeline without checks.

1 Click **View As** next to **Review what other people see on your Timeline?** to check what anyone selecting your Timeline is shown

2 Click **Edit** next to **Who can see posts you've been tagged in on your Timeline?** and make a choice from the audience selector. Selecting Only me will ensure any posts you are tagged in are hidden

3 Click **Edit** next to **Who can see what others post on your Timeline?** and make a choice from the audience selector. Again, selecting Only me will ensure any posts you are tagged in are hidden

Manage tags people add

1 If someone adds a tag to your post, it allows the person tagged and their friends to see the post. To stop this happening automatically, click **Edit** next to **Review tags people add to your own posts before the tags appear on Facebook?** and select Enabled. You'll now be asked to review it first

2 Click **Edit** next to **When you're tagged in a post, who do you want to add to the audience if they aren't already in it?** Select Only me, Friends or Custom

3 When someone uploads a photo that looks like you, they may see your name as a suggested tag. You can turn it off by clicking **Edit** next to **Who sees tag suggestions when photos that look like you are uploaded?**

Hot tip

Click Edit List next to Restricted List if you want to unblock people. Simply click on their names again.

Blocking users and apps

If you don't want certain friends to see your posts or if you want to block invites, Pages and apps, you can easily do on the Manage Blocking page.

1 Click the Question Mark icon in the top-right corner, and select **Settings**

2 Click **Blocking** from the left-hand menu

What you can manage

● **Restricted List:** You can add friends to a Restricted List, which means they will only see your Public posts or items posted on a mutual friend's Timeline. Click **Edit List** next to **Restricted List**, and either search for people or select Friends from the drop-down menu, and click the names of those you want to add to it.

● **Block people:** You can block specific people and prevent them from interacting with you, except in

Block users [Add name or email] [Block]

Groups where you are both members. Include the name or email address of people you want to ban in the section **Block Users**, and click **Block**.

● **Block messages, app invites and event invites:** You will see three sections marked

Block invites from [Type the name of a friend...]

Block messages, **Block app invites** and **Block event invites**. Type the name of a friend into any of these boxes to block someone from performing the action.

● **Block apps and Pages:** Type the name of an app or Page into the box within the sections for **Block apps** and **Block Pages**, and the apps will not be able to grab non-public information about you or contact you, while the Pages will be unable to interact with your posts or comments. By doing this, you'd automatically unfollow and unlike a page.

Enhancing mobile privacy

Since you are likely to use Facebook on your mobile rather heavily, you should configure the settings on your device for better privacy.

Better privacy in iOS

1 Tap the **Settings** app from your iOS device's Home screen

Hot tip

Turning off Location will prevent Facebook from sharing your whereabouts when you post something.

2 Keep scrolling until you see the entry for **Facebook**. Tap it

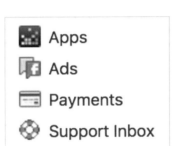

3 Select **Settings**

4 Go down the list of things that Facebook is allowed to access. Move the green sliders to off if you want to stop Facebook accessing that particular feature. You can stop Facebook accessing your Photos, Microphone and Camera. You can also stop the app refreshing in the background, and prevent it from using your mobile data and sending you notifications

Better privacy in Android

1 Tap the **Settings** app

2 Tap **Apps**

3 Select **Facebook**

4 Tap **Permissions**

5 Toggle the switches next to various features to turn them on and off, as with iOS in Step 4 above

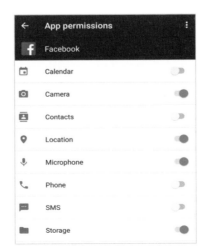

Hot tip

You can also click the downward arrow on any post you see on your Timeline, and select Remove Tag if you are tagged within it.

Hot tip

The ability to untag and report posts and images is also available within the app. Simply tap the downward arrow in the right-hand corner of a post, and select Remove Tag.

Remove tags from photos

If you allow yourself to be tagged by others, you may end up being tagged in a photo or post that you'd rather wasn't flagged up in such a way. You can remove the tags very easily.

1 Click the downward arrow in the top-right of the screen

2 Select **Activity Log**

3 Select **Tag Review** from the left-hand menu. If there are no tags to review, click **Timeline Review**

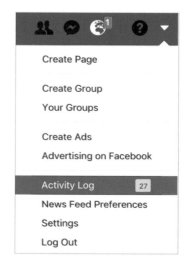

4 Go down the list to find images and posts that you want to be untagged from

5 Select the downward arrow to the right of a post, and click **Remove Tag**

6 The tag will then be removed

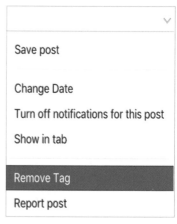

7 You may also feel that the post in which you were included is offensive in some way. If this is the case, then go through the same steps 1 to 4 as above, but click **Report post**

8 You will then be asked to explain why you are reporting the post. Select the reason and select **Continue**, filling in any other forms that Facebook asks for

Add extra login security

As well as changing your password often, you should consider adding two-factor authentication. This means, in addition to using a password, you are sent a code to your phone that you also have to input. It helps prevent anyone else from logging in, since they'd need to know your login details and have possession of your phone.

1 Click the downward arrow in the top-right of the screen, and select **Settings**

2 Select **Security and Login** from the left-hand menu

3 Scroll down to the section Setting up extra security, and select **Edit** next to **Use two-factor authentication**

4 Click **Add phone number** next to Text Message (SMS) if you haven't already

5 Click **Set up**, and select **Enable**

> Two-factor authentication is off.   Set Up
> Add an extra layer of security to prevent other people from logging into your account. Learn More

6 Re-enter your Facebook password, and click **Close** when prompted. Now when you log in, a code will be sent to your phone which you need to use to gain access

7 You'll be asked if you want Facebook to remember your devices, ensuring codes are only needed in addition to passwords when you (or someone else) tries to log into Facebook via an unrecognized device

> **Set Up Two-Factor Authentication?**   ⊠
>
> Are you sure you want to set up two-factor authentication?
> ✓ For the next seven days, do not require a second factor to turn off two-factor authentication.
>
>   Cancel   **Enable**

179

Hot tip

If you do receive an alert and you do not recognize the device or browser, always change your password.

Get suspicious login alerts

If Facebook detects someone has logged in on a device or browser that you do not normally use, you can receive an alert.

1 Click the downward arrow in the top-right of the screen, and select **Settings**

2 Select **Security and Login** from the left-hand menu

3 Scroll down to the section Setting up extra security and select **Edit** next to **Get alerts about unrecognized logins**

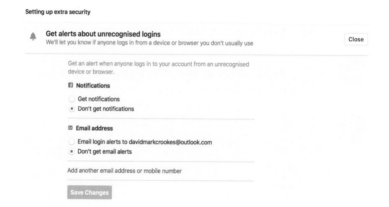

4 If you want the alert to be a Facebook notification, select the button next to **Get notifications**

5 If you want the alert to be sent to your email address, click the button next to **Email login alerts to...**

6 You can change the email address by clicking **Add another email address or mobile number**

7 Click **Save Changes**

Tackling a hacked account

Unfortunately, some people set up fake Facebook accounts in other people's names or manage to hack into an existing account. If this happens to you, there are some steps you can take.

Dealing with an imposter account

1 If you discover somebody is using your email address or phone number on an account that you have not set up, simply add that email address or phone number to your own account, and it will be removed from the other

2 If you discover somebody is pretending to be you, then visit the offending profile, click the three-dot button on its cover photo, and select **Report**. Now tell Facebook about your suspicions

Dealing with a hacked account

1 Should your account be compromised, go to **http://www.facebook.com/hacked**

2 Click **Get Started**, and Facebook will perform checks on your account before taking you through the process of securing it

Ending an active hacking session

1 What if somebody is accessing your account right now? Click the downward arrow in the top-right corner, and select **Settings**

2 Click **Security and login** in the left-hand menu

3 Look under the heading **Where you're logged in**. Click the three-button option to the right of the entries, and select **Log out** or click **Log out of all sessions**

It may be worth telling your friends that you believe you have been hacked, in case they have received any messages from the hacker or seen anything untoward on your account.

Hot tip

Only your friends will be able to see that you are safe, so don't worry about broadcasting your whereabouts to the wider public.

Mark yourself as safe

The world is not always as safe as it should be. Terrorism, natural disasters and terrifying incidents may touch our lives at any time. It can lead others to worry about your safety, regardless of whether you are in the midst of the crisis or simply in the vicinity. To help relieve stress and worry among your friends and family, Facebook has a Safety Check feature which allows you to indicate that you are okay. The function is activated by the Facebook community when an incident occurs. It will appear if a lot of people are discussing the incident in a particular area.

1 If you are in an affected area, Facebook will look at the area you have listed in your profile, determine if you are using the internet in that location and send you a message asking if you are safe

2 You are then given two options: **I'm safe** and **I'm not in the area**. You can select the most appropriate

3 If you mark yourself as safe, then this information will appear on your friends' News Feeds, and a notification will also be sent

4 Doing so can put other people's minds at ease, letting them know that you are okay. Likewise, you will be able to see if other people you know are safe too

14 Using third-party apps

This brief chapter helps you make more of Facebook.

If you log in to a service using Facebook and later decide you don't want to do this, search online to see if the company will let you switch to a standard login. Some, such as Spotify, have help pages detailing such a process.

When signing up to an app or game, look for the button Edit This on the screen, which shows the information the app is set to receive. You can remove some of that information. See the opposite page for details of what can be changed. As you'll see, you can alter the app settings at any time.

Using Facebook as a login

Many websites and apps allow you to bypass the tedium of setting up a username and password in order to access them. Instead, they let you log in using your Facebook credentials, saving time and cutting the hassle of having to keep remembering your details.

Services that allow you to do this include music-streaming site Spotify, restaurant reservation service OpenTable, and the image-collecting network Pinterest. In fact, social logins have almost become the norm, so you are bound to encounter them at one point or another. Many love the modern convenience on offer.

Should I use it?

Facebook wants to be a trusted source for verifying your identity.

- It will never give the third party your Facebook password.

- It lets you benefit from its advanced security, which means it is more secure when logging into small websites.

- It puts you in control, allowing you to delete your account with the third party with ease.

- But Facebook will typically provide the third party with your public profile (which means your name, profile picture, age range, gender, language and country) as well as your Friends list, email address and date of birth.

Signing up to a third-party service using Facebook

1 Taking Spotify as an example, go to **http://www.spotify.com** and click **Sign up**. You'll see the option **Sign up with Facebook**

2 Click this, and you can get around filling in your email address, password and date of birth. Click **Continue**

3 Now you'll be able to simply select **Log in with Facebook** to access the service in future

Altering the app settings

You can fine-tune what you share with third-party apps. The only exception is that you are unable to prevent them from seeing your name, profile picture, cover photo, gender, networks, username and user ID.

Changing the permissions for third-party apps

1 Click the downward arrow in the top right-hand corner of the screen, and select **Settings**

2 Click **Apps** from the left-hand menu

3 Any apps you have logged into using Facebook appear at the top of the screen. Select the one you want to look at in greater detail

4 Select the drop-down, **Friends**, and decide who can see that you use the app

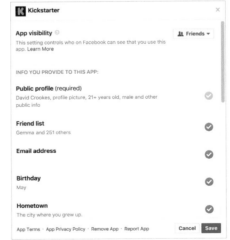

5 You will see a list of information you are providing to the app. Untick anything you want to stop

6 Scroll down further, and choose whether or not you want the app to send you notifications through Facebook

7 Click **Save**

Hot tip

Remove apps you don't use any more by hovering over them in the Settings and clicking the **X** delete button.

By selecting Edit in the box Apps Others Use, you can alter the information your friends are able to see about you, such as your birthday, app activity and current city.

Controlling apps and games

You can change the settings in Facebook to prevent you from being able to log into websites, applications or games using Facebook. You can also stop friends interacting with you using apps and websites.

1 Click the downward arrow in the top right-hand corner of the screen, and select **Settings**

2 Click **Apps** from the left-hand menu

3 Select **Edit** in the box marked Apps, Websites and Plugins

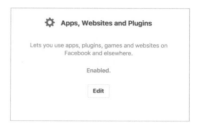

⚙ **Apps, Websites and Plugins**

Lets you use apps, plugins, games and websites on Facebook and elsewhere.

Enabled.

Edit

4 Select **Disable Platform**

Stop game requests and app notifications
If you are fed up receiving invites to games such as Candy Crush Saga, you can call a halt to them.

1 Again, click the downward arrow in the top right-hand corner of the screen, and select **Settings**. Click **Apps**

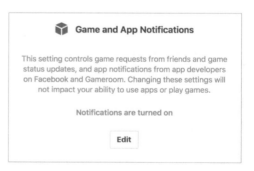

📦 **Game and App Notifications**

This setting controls game requests from friends and game status updates, and app notifications from app developers on Facebook and Gameroom. Changing these settings will not impact your ability to use apps or play games.

Notifications are turned on

Edit

2 Click **Edit** in the box called Game and App Notifications

3 Select **Turn Off**

Index

Symbols

A

B

C

D

E

F

G

H

I

K

L

M

Q

R

S

T

V

WITHDRAWN

W

Y

$15.99   11/28/17

Z